# FREE

## Free Study Tips DVD

In addition to the tips and content in this guide, we have created a FREE DVD with helpful study tips to further assist your exam preparation. **This FREE Study Tips DVD provides you with top-notch tips to conquer your exam and reach your goals.**

Our simple request in exchange for the strategy-packed DVD is that you email us your feedback about our study guide. We would love to hear what you thought about the guide, and we welcome any and all feedback—positive, negative, or neutral. It is our #1 goal to provide you with top-quality products and customer service.

To receive your **FREE Study Tips DVD**, email freedvd@apexprep.com. Please put "FREE DVD" in the subject line and put the following in the email:

     a. The name of the study guide you purchased.

     b. Your rating of the study guide on a scale of 1-5, with 5 being the highest score.

     c. Any thoughts or feedback about your study guide.

     d. Your first and last name and your mailing address, so we know where to send your free DVD!

Thank you!

# IELTS General Training and Academic Exam Preparation

IELTS Book with Practice Test Questions
[Includes Audio Links for Listening Section Prep]

Matthew Lanni

Written and edited by APEX Publishing.

ISBN 13: 9781637754573
ISBN 10: 1637754574

APEX Publishing is not connected with or endorsed by any official testing organization. APEX Publishing creates and publishes unofficial educational products. All test and organization names are trademarks of their respective owners.

The material in this publication is included for utilitarian purposes only and does not constitute an endorsement by APEX Publishing of any particular point of view.

For additional information or for bulk orders, contact info@apexprep.com.

# Table of Contents

# Test Taking Strategies

## 1. Reading the Whole Question

A popular assumption in Western culture is the idea that we don't have enough time for anything. We speed while driving to work, we want to read an assignment for class as quickly as possible, or we want the line in the supermarket to dwindle faster. However, speeding through such events robs us from being able to thoroughly appreciate and understand what's happening around us. While taking a timed test, the feeling one might have while reading a question is to find the correct answer as quickly as possible. Although pace is important, don't let it deter you from reading the whole question. Test writers know how to subtly change a test question toward the end in various ways, such as adding a negative or changing focus. If the question has a passage, carefully read the whole passage as well before moving on to the questions. This will help you process the information in the passage rather than worrying about the questions you've just read and where to find them. A thorough understanding of the passage or question is an important way for test takers to be able to succeed on an exam.

## 2. Examining Every Answer Choice

Let's say we're at the market buying apples. The first apple we see on top of the heap may *look* like the best apple, but if we turn it over we can see bruising on the skin. We must examine several apples before deciding which apple is the best. Finding the correct answer choice is like finding the best apple. Some exams ask for the *best* answer choice, which means that there are several choices that could be correct, but one choice is always better than the rest. Although it's tempting to choose an answer that seems correct at first without reading the others, it's important to read each answer choice thoroughly before making a final decision on the answer. The aim of a test writer might be to get as close as possible to the correct answer, so watch out for subtle words that may indicate an answer is incorrect. Once the correct answer choice is selected, read the question again and the answer in response to make sure all your bases are covered.

## 3. Eliminating Wrong Answer Choices

Sometimes we become paralyzed when we are confronted with too many choices. Which frozen yogurt flavor is the tastiest? Which pair of shoes look the best with this outfit? What type of car will fill my needs as a consumer? If you are unsure of which answer would be the best to choose, it may help to use process of elimination. We use "filtering" all the time on sites such as eBay® or Craigslist® to eliminate the ads that are not right for us. We can do the same thing on an exam. Process of elimination is crossing out the answer choices we know for sure are wrong and leaving the ones that might be correct. It may help to cover up the incorrect answer choices with a piece of paper, although if the exam is computer-based, you may have to use your hand or mentally cross out the incorrect answer choices. Covering incorrect choices is a psychological act that alleviates stress due to the brain being exposed to a smaller amount of information. Choosing between two answer choices is much easier than choosing between four or five, and you have a better chance of selecting the correct answer if you have less to focus on.

## 4. Sticking to the World of the Question

When we are attempting to answer questions, our minds will often wander away from the question and what it is asking. We begin to see answer choices that are true in the real world instead of true in the world of the question. It may be helpful to think of each test question as its own little world. This world may be different from ours. This world may know as a truth that the chicken came before the egg or may assert that two plus two equals five. Remember that, no matter what hypothetical nonsense may be in the question, assume it to be true. If the question states that the chicken came before the egg, then choose your answer based on that truth. Sticking to the world of the question means placing all of our biases and assumptions aside and relying on the question to guide us to the correct answer. If we are simply looking for answers that are correct based on our own judgment, then we may choose incorrectly. Remember an answer that is true does not necessarily answer the question.

## 5. Key Words

If you come across a complex test question that you have to read over and over again, try pulling out some key words from the question in order to understand what exactly it is asking. Key words may be words that surround the question, such as *main idea, analogous, parallel, resembles, structured,* or *defines.* The question may be asking for the main idea, or it may be asking you to define something. Deconstructing the sentence may also be helpful in making the question simpler before trying to answer it. This means taking the sentence apart and obtaining meaning in pieces, or separating the question from the foundation of the question. For example, let's look at this question:

> Given the author's description of the content of paleontology in the first paragraph, which of the following is most parallel to what it taught?

The question asks which one of the answers most *parallels* the following information: The *description* of paleontology in the first paragraph. The first step would be to see *how* paleontology is described in the first paragraph. Then, we would find an answer choice that parallels that description. The question seems complex at first, but after we deconstruct it, the answer becomes much more attainable.

## 6. Subtle Negatives

Negative words in question stems will be words such as *not, but, neither,* or *except.* Test writers often use these words in order to trick unsuspecting test takers into selecting the wrong answer—or, at least, to test their reading comprehension of the question. Many exams will feature the negative words in all caps (*which of the following is NOT an example*), but some questions will add the negative word seamlessly into the sentence. The following is an example of a subtle negative used in a question stem:

> According to the passage, which of the following is *not* considered to be an example of paleontology?

If we rush through the exam, we might skip that tiny word, *not,* inside the question, and choose an answer that is opposite of the correct choice. Again, it's important to read the question fully, and double check for any words that may negate the statement in any way.

## 7. Spotting the Hedges

The word "hedging" refers to language that remains vague or avoids absolute terminology. Absolute terminology consists of words like *always, never, all, every, just, only, none,* and *must.* Hedging refers to words like *seem, tend, might, most, some, sometimes, perhaps, possibly, probability,* and *often.* In some cases, we want to choose answer choices that use hedging and avoid answer choices that use absolute terminology. Of course, this always depends on what subject you are being tested on. Humanities subjects like history and literature will contain hedging, because those subjects often do not have absolute answers. However, science and math may contain absolutes that are necessary for the question to be answered. It's important to pay attention to what subject you are on and adjust your response accordingly.

## 8. Restating to Understand

Every now and then we come across questions that we don't understand. The language may be too complex, or the question is structured in a way that is meant to confuse the test taker. When you come across a question like this, it may be worth your time to rewrite or restate the question in your own words in order to understand it better. For example, let's look at the following complicated question:

> Which of the following words, if substituted for the word *parochial* in the first paragraph, would LEAST change the meaning of the sentence?

Let's restate the question in order to understand it better. We know that they want the word *parochial* replaced. We also know that this new word would "least" or "not" change the meaning of the sentence. Now let's try the sentence again:

> Which word could we replace with *parochial,* and it would not change the meaning?

Restating it this way, we see that the question is asking for a synonym. Now, let's restate the question so we can answer it better:

> Which word is a synonym for the word *parochial?*

Before we even look at the answer choices, we have a simpler, restated version of a complicated question. Remember that, if you have paper, you can always rewrite the simpler version of the question so as not to forget it.

## 9. Guessing

When is it okay to guess on an exam? This question depends on the test format of the particular exam you're taking. On some tests, answer choices that are answered incorrectly are penalized. If you know that you are penalized for wrong answer choices, avoid guessing on the test question. If you can narrow the question down to fifty percent by process of elimination, then perhaps it may be worth it to guess between two answer choices. But if you are unsure of the correct answer choice among three or four answers, it may help to leave the question unanswered. Likewise, if the exam you are taking does *not* penalize for wrong answer choices, answer the questions first you know to be true, then go back through and mark an answer choice, even if you do not know the correct answer. This way, you will at least have a one in four chance of getting the answer correct. It may also be helpful to do some research on the exam you plan to take in order to understand how the questions are graded.

## 10. Avoiding Patterns

One popular myth in grade school relating to standardized testing is that test writers will often put multiple-choice answers in patterns. A runoff example of this kind of thinking is that the most common answer choice is "C," with "B" following close behind. Or, some will advocate certain made-up word patterns that simply do not exist. Test writers do not arrange their correct answer choices in any kind of pattern; their choices are randomized. There may even be times where the correct answer choice will be the same letter for two or three questions in a row, but we have no way of knowing when or if this might happen. Instead of trying to figure out what choice the test writer probably set as being correct, focus on what the *best answer choice* would be out of the answers you are presented with. Use the tips above, general knowledge, and reading comprehension skills in order to best answer the question, rather than looking for patterns that do not exist.

# FREE DVD OFFER

Achieving a high score on your exam depends not only on understanding the content, but also on understanding how to apply your knowledge and your command of test taking strategies. **Because your success is our primary goal, we offer a FREE Study Tips DVD. It provides top-notch test taking strategies to help you optimize your testing experience.**

Our simple request in exchange for the strategy-packed DVD is that you email us your feedback about our study guide.

To receive your **FREE Study Tips DVD**, email freedvd@apexprep.com. Please put "FREE DVD" in the subject line and put the following in the email:

> a. The name of the study guide you purchased.
>
> b. Your rating of the study guide on a scale of 1-5, with 5 being the highest score.
>
> c. Any thoughts or feedback about your study guide.
>
> d. Your first and last name and your mailing address, so we know where to send your free DVD!

# Introduction

**Function of the Test**

The International English Language Testing System (IELTS) is an exam that students or professionals take in order to measure their level of proficiency in English. Those looking to take the IELTS are often migrating to countries where English is widely used, or they seek to work within a setting that uses the English language frequently. Countries that accept the IELTS exam are Australia, New Zealand, Canada, the U.K., and the U.S.A, although they have their own requirements for the exam.

**Test Administration**

There are two types of IELTS exam: the IELTS Academic and the IELTS General Training. The IELTS Academic exam is for individuals who are applying to higher education programs at an English-speaking university or a professional registration in an English-speaking atmosphere. The IELTS General Training is for individuals applying to secondary education, work, or training programs, and it is also required for migration to Canada, New Zealand, Australia, and the U.K.

Retesting is available to individuals who fail all or part of the exam, but the entire IELTS must be taken again. For individuals with special requirements, including medical conditions, learning difficulties, hearing/visual difficulties, or infant feeding, alert the testing center before sitting the exam. If you require a modified exam, alert three months prior. If you require special arrangements, alert six weeks prior.

**Test Format**

The IELTS Academic and IELTS General Training both may be taken either on paper or on computer. For paper exams, individuals will take the Reading, Listening, and Writing sections at an official IELTS test center. The Speaking section will be carried out in-person with an IELTS examiner. For computer exams, individuals will take the Reading, Listening, and Writing sections on a computer, but the Speaking section is carried out in-person with an IELTS examiner.

There are four sections in the IELTS Academic and IELTS General Training: Listening, Reading, Writing, and Speaking. Although Listening and Speaking are the same for both exams, the content in the Reading and Writing sections differ. In all, each section has the same time limit and number of questions, as shown below. The total time to take the exam is two hours and forty-five minutes.

| IELTS Academic and General Training | | |
|---|---|---|
| Listening | 30 minutes | 40 questions |
| Reading | 60 minutes | 40 questions |
| Writing | 60 minutes | 2 questions |
| Speaking | 11–14 minutes | 3 parts |

**Scoring**

The IELTS uses band scores that scale from 1 to 9. Score of 1 is considered a non-user, where the test taker has knowledge of a few isolated words, but no ability to speak the language. Score of 9 is considered an expert, where the test taker has full fluency of the language.

# Listening

## General Format

The Listening section of the IELTS takes a total of two hours and forty-five minutes. The assessors of the IELTS exam are looking for test takers' ability to follow the main idea of a conversation or lecture, to gather the factual information, to assess the opinions and attitudes of the speakers, and to understanding how ideas develop within a conversation or monologue.

For the first thirty minutes of the exam, four recordings will be provided for test takers to listen to. Each of the recordings are done by native English speakers. The first recording depicts two people having a conversation in a daily social context. The second recording is a monologue or speech by a single person pertaining to an everyday social context. The third recording involves up to 4 people in an academic or training setting having a conversation about an assignment or project. The fourth recording depicts a monologue in an academic setting, such as a college lecture.

Each recording will have ten questions each, and the questions will be in the same order as test takers hear the recordings. Test takers are only able to hear the recordings once each. A variety of accents will be represented, including British, Australian, New Zealand, American, and Canadian.

The question types are multiple choice, matching, plan/map/diagram labeling, form/note/table/flow-chart/summary completion, and sentence completion. Each question will be worth one point each. The exam is assessed by certified markers who are checked for reliability on a regular basis. Even after these certified markers check the exam, it is analyzed further by Cambridge Assessment English.

## Task Types

### Multiple Choice
The **multiple-choice questions** present a single question and gives you three multiple-choice answers to choose from. Or, the question will ask you to complete the blank, and you will have three answers that are potential endings to that blank. The choices are represented by *A, B,* and *C.* Every now and then the question will require test takers to choose *more than one* answer choice. Read every question carefully to assess how many answers you are required to choose. Multiple-choice questions require test takers to have a detailed understanding of specific points listed within the recording.

### Matching
**Matching question** types are used to determine if test takers can follow along and pick up important details spoken in an everyday conversation, and whether or not a test taker can follow along a conversation spoken in a second language. The matching question format involves a numbered list of items beside the recordings. The test taker must then match that list to a set of options given on the question paper.

### Plan, Map, Diagram Labelling
The **plan, map, and diagram labelling task type** requires test takers to fill in labels on a plan, map, or diagram. The answers will be listed on the question paper for test takers to choose from. This task type analyzes the ability of the test taker to understanding specific details of a place and then transfer this knowledge to a visual representation. Test takers must have a solid understanding of directions and spatial relationships to successfully complete this task type.

## Form, Note, Table, Flow-Chart, Summary Completion

The **form, note, table, flow-chart, and summary completion task type** presents an outline of part of the recording and requires test takers to fill in the gaps on the paper. Main ideas and facts are most often presented in this outline. The missing items in the outline will either be gaps on paper or gaps in the recording, though words from the recording should not be changed. The specific number of words needed will be detailed in each question, so read the directions carefully. If test takers write more words than the stated amount, their answers will be marked incorrect. Contracted words are not tested, and hyphenated words count as single words. The following are types of charts the test may include:

- A form to record factual details, such as names or places
- A set of notes showing how different items relate to each other in a layout format
- A table to summarize information into coherent categories
- A flow-chart to summarize the stages of a process shown by arrows

## Sentence Completion

In the **sentence completion task**, test takers are given a set of sentences to read from the recording. The sentences usually summarize important information from the recording. Test takers are then asked to fill in a gap in each sentence from the knowledge they gathered from the recording. A specific word limit is always given in these tasks. Test takers must be careful to write only the amount of words given in the directions. The skills tested in this task are identifying important information from a recording as well as instances of cause and effect.

## Short-Answer Questions

In the **short-answer task**, test takers are given a question and then asked to write an open-ended answer to the question. Information from the recording will be used in this task. A word limit is given for this task also, and some test takers will be penalized for writing more than the suggested word count. Again, contracted words will not be tested, and hyphenated words count as single words. Every now and then the question will ask test takers to make a list in three points as the answer. This task measures the ability of test takers to remember important facts such as people, places, prices, or times given in the recording.

## Test Strategies

### Reading Questions

Before test takers begin the IELTS Listening recording, they should read over the questions first. The recording can only be listened to one time, and then after that, test takers must rely on their memories only to complete the questions. If test takers skim the information beforehand, they are at an advantage because they will know what to listen for while the recording is playing and thus be more confident filling in the task types afterward. Reading beforehand is important because test takers are also allowed to take notes during the recordings. Given this information, test takers can mark down correct answers before the recording ends.

### Taking Notes

Some test takers will be better at multitasking than others. Although taking notes during the recording requires test takers to use two skills at once, writing and listening, some test takers *listen better* when they are able to write down the information being spoken because they are focused on the information and writing it down rather than zoning out. Taking notes will help many test takers answer questions correctly. One suggestion would be to take notes only when tedious details are offered in the recording. Write down the names of names, places, prices, or any other kind of factual information that can be jotted down in a second.

## Practicing Listening

Listening is an active skill—it requires more than simply *hearing* what someone says. Listening is retaining information and then analyzing that information to make sense of the conversation as a whole. Listening involves the whole body. Those who are good listeners will turn their bodies toward the speaker or recording and focus on what the speaker is saying without formulating a response or judgment in the mind. There are unlimited recordings of online lectures or people offering instructions to those in need. Search the internet for a recording you can listen to and then practice taking notes of that recording. Listen with the whole body and become actively interested in what the speaker is saying. Try to do one recording a day and you will see a difference in the way you respond to future conversations.

## Guessing

Test takers should guess when they are taking the IELTS Listening section, because points are not taken off for incorrect answers. One strategy would be to leave all uncertain questions to be finished at the end, and then go back and put in the closest guess that you have. Remember to still pay attention to the word count, because markers will penalize if the word count does not line up with the instructions. Even if test takers don't absolutely know the correct answer, there's always a chance they could guess and get it right!

## Checking Spelling and Grammar

Test takers should always check their work before handing in the finished test. People who assess the Listening section will take off for incorrect grammar and spelling. Therefore, it's crucial that test takers read over their work carefully to catch any mistakes they may have made. If test takers are unsure their spelling is correct, they should do their best and leave the answer filled in. Remember that blank answers will receive no credit, but there is always a chance the test taker will spell the word correctly or get partial credit for a misspelled word.

# Reading

## Types of Questions

### Multiple Choice

**Multiple-choice questions** test your understanding of a single part of the passage or the main point of the entire passage. These questions either ask you how to best complete a sentence, or they ask you for the best answer to a question. Multiple Choice questions appear in the order in which the information is presented in the passage. For example, a question about the first sentence will appear before a question about the second sentence.

Each question provides a series of answer choices. Depending on the question, there might be four, five, or seven answer choices, and they are always labeled A, B, C, D, E, F, or G. When there are four answer choices, you need to choose the single best answer. When there are five answer choices, you need to choose the two best answers. When there are seven answer choices, you need to choose the best three answers. When narrowing down answer choices, remember that the best answer choices are the ones that have the most support in the passage.

### Identifying Information

**Identifying information questions** test your understanding of the passage. The questions provide a statement and ask whether the passage supports it. The answer choices are True, False, and Not Given. If the statement is supported by the passage, then the answer is True. If the statement is refuted by the passage, then the answer is False. If the statement is not mentioned by the passage, then the answer is Not Given.

You should use the passage only to answer Identifying Information questions; do not rely on any other knowledge. For example, if you know the statement is true based on your personal knowledge but the passage does not mention it, then you should choose the answer Not Given. Identifying Information questions appear in the same order in which the information is presented in the passage.

### Identifying Writer's Views or Claims

**Identifying writer's views or claims questions** test your understanding of the opinions or arguments of the passage's author. These questions provide you with a statement and then ask whether that statement is consistent with the author's views or claims. These questions ask whether the author would agree with the statement. The answer choices are Yes, No, or Not Given. If the author would agree with the statement, then the answer is Yes. If the author would disagree with the statement, then the answer is No. If the passage does not contain the author's view on the statement, then the answer is Not Given.

As with the Identifying Information questions, you should not use any outside knowledge to answer these questions. These questions typically appear in passages that contain arguments, and the questions appear in the same order in which the information is presented in the passage.

### Matching Information

**Matching information questions** test your ability to retrieve information from the passage. The questions provide you with a definition, example, fact, opinion, reasoning, summary, or some other piece of information from the passage, and then they ask you to match it to a paragraph. The passage's paragraphs are labeled with a letter of the alphabet, and these letters function as the answer choices.

Some paragraphs do not contain an answer choice, while others might contain multiple correct answers. If a paragraph contains multiple correct answers, the instructions tell you that a paragraph letter can be used more than one time. Matching information questions do not appear in the order in which the information is presented in the passage.

## Matching Headings

**Matching headings questions** test your ability to understand the main ideas of the paragraphs. Each paragraph is labeled with a letter in alphabetical order, and you are provided with a list of headings labeled with a Roman numeral number (i, ii, iii, iv, v, vi, and so on). The headings include a short description, and you will need to match those descriptions with the paragraphs. The purpose is to test whether you can distinguish between main ideas, supporting ideas, and themes.

No heading is ever used for multiple paragraphs. In addition, the test always provides more headings than paragraphs. So some of the headings will be left unused. Sometimes the test provides the headings for some of the paragraphs as examples. If that is the case, then the headings given as answer choices are not used for paragraphs that already have a heading.

## Matching Features

**Matching features questions** test your ability to spot relationships and make connections based on information contained in the passage. In addition, these questions test your ability to retrieve information, because they require you to find a series of items in the passage. The test provides a statement for you to match with something described in the passage. Your options are identified with a letter of the alphabet. For example, if the passage describes several politicians and you are provided with a statement about an accomplishment, then you would match the accomplishment to the politician.

Some of the options might be left unused, and the instructions will let you know if that is the case. Matching Features questions might appear in passages with facts, descriptions, or narratives. These questions do not appear in the same order in which the information is presented in the passage.

## Matching Sentence Endings

**Matching sentence endings questions** test your ability to understand important concepts contained in the passage. Like some types of Multiple Choice questions, Matching Sentence questions provide an incomplete sentence and then ask what answer choice best completes it. However, unlike Multiple Choice questions, the answer choices will be provided as a list that applies to multiple Matching Sentence questions. The answer choices will be labeled with a letter of the alphabet. Your job is to choose the answer choice that best completes each sentence. There will always be more options in the list than the number of Matching Sentence questions. So if there are multiple answer choices that seem to fit, you should choose the answer choice that is the strongest.

Since Matching Sentence questions test main points and important concepts, they can appear in almost any type of passage. These questions appear in the same order in which the information is presented in the passage.

## Sentence Completion

**Sentence completion questions** test your ability to find specific details in the passage. Like some Multiple Choice questions and Matching Sentence Endings questions, these questions include an incomplete sentence. However, Sentence Completion questions ask you to write the answer on the answer sheet. The correct answer is usually a specific concept or figure. Sentence Completion questions appear in the same order in which the information is presented in the passage.

The instructions state in capital letters how many words or numbers your answer should include. For example, the instructions might read "ONE WORD ONLY" or "NO MORE THAN TWO WORDS." Answers are typically three words or less. You can write numbers as a word or a number, and hyphenated words are counted as one word. The answer will not include a contraction, like *won't* or *wouldn't.* If you write more words or numbers than are asked for, your answer is incorrect.

## Summary, Note, Table, Flow-Chart Completion

**Summary, note, table, flow-chart completion questions** test your ability to understand details and main ideas from the passage. These questions come in four different forms: several sentences, several notes, a table with multiple rows or columns, or a series of steps linked by arrows in a sequence. Regardless of the form, you need to fill in what has been left blank.

Some of the questions include a list of answer choices, and others tell you to use the passage. When you need to use the passage, the instructions state in capital letters how many words or numbers your answer should consist of. For example, the instructions might read "ONE WORD ONLY" or "NO MORE THAN TWO WORDS." Answers are typically three words or less. You can write numbers as a word or a numeral ("four" or "4"), and hyphenated words are counted as one word. The answer will not include a contraction, such as *won't* or *wouldn't.* If you write more words or numbers than are asked for, your answer is incorrect.

## Diagram Label Completion

**Diagram label completion questions** test your ability to process information contained in the passage and then place it on a diagram. In the provided diagram, some part is left blank, and you need to write out your answer. Diagrams are often based on a single descriptive part of the passage. For example, if the passage is about a famous architect, the diagram might illustrate features from the architect's most famous work.

The instructions state in capital letters how many words or numbers your answer should consist of. For example, the instructions might read "ONE WORD ONLY" or "NO MORE THAN TWO WORDS." Answers are typically three words or less. You can write numbers as a word or a numeral ("four" or "4"), and hyphenated words are counted as one word. The answer will not include a contraction, like *won't* or *wouldn't.* If you write more words than are asked for, your answer is incorrect.

## Short Answer

**Short-answer questions** test your ability to find and understand factual information contained in the passage. The questions ask for a specific detail, and you need to write out your answers. Because the answer needs to be short and specific, the correct answer is usually an important concept or figure. Short-Answer questions appear in the same order in which the information is presented in the passage.

The instructions state in capital letters how many words or numbers your answer should consist of. For example, the instructions might read "ONE WORD ONLY" or "NO MORE THAN TWO WORDS." Answers are typically three words or less. You can write numbers as or a numeral ("four" or "4"), and hyphenated words are counted as one word. The answer will not include a contraction, like *won't* or *wouldn't.* If you write more words than are asked for, your answer is incorrect.

## Identifying Specific Information from a Printed Communication

### Business Memos

Whereas everyday **office memos** were traditionally typed on paper, photocopied, and distributed, today they are more often typed on computers and distributed via email, both interoffice and externally. Technology has thus made these communications more immediate. It is also helpful for people to read carefully and be familiar with memo components. For example, emails automatically provide the same "To:, From:, and Re:" lines traditionally required in paper memos, and in corresponding places—the top of the page/screen. Readers should observe whether "To: names/positions" include all intended recipients in case of misdirection errors or omitted recipients. "From:" informs sender level, role, and who will receive responses when people click "Reply." Users must be careful not to click "Reply All" unintentionally. They should also observe the "CC:" line, typically below "Re:," showing additional recipients.

## Classified Ads

**Classified advertisements** include "Help Wanted" ads informing readers of positions open for hiring, real estate listings, cars for sale, and home and business services available. Traditional ads in newspapers had to save space, and this necessity has largely transferred to online ads. Because of needing to save space, advertisers employ many abbreviations. For example, here are some examples of abbreviations:

- FT=full-time
- PT=part-time
- A/P=accounts payable
- A/R=accounts receivable
- Asst.=assistant
- Bkkg.=bookkeeping
- Comm.=commission
- Bet.=between
- EOE=equal opportunity employer
- G/L=general ledger
- Immed.=immediately
- Exc.=excellent
- Exp.=experience
- Eves.=evenings
- Secy.=secretary
- Temp=temporary
- Sal=salary
- Req=required
- Refs=references
- Wk=week or work
- WPM=words per minute

Classified ads frequently use abbreviations to take up less space, both on paper and digitally on websites. Those who read these ads will find it less confusing if they learn some common abbreviations used by businesses when advertising job positions. Here are some examples:

- Mgt.=management
- Mgr.=manager
- Mfg.=manufacturing
- Nat'l=national
- Dept.=department
- Min.=minimum
- Yrs.=years
- Nec=necessary
- Neg=negotiable
- Oppty=opportunity

- O/T=overtime
- K=1,000

Readers of classified ads may focus on certain features to the exclusion of others. For example, if a reader sees the job title or salary they are seeking, or notices the experience, education, degree, or other credentials required match their own qualifications perfectly, they may fail to notice other important information, like "No benefits." This is important because the employers are disclosing that they will not provide health insurance, retirement accounts, paid sick leave, paid maternity/paternity leave, paid vacation, etc. to any employee whom they hire. Someone expecting a traditional 9 to 5 job who fails to observe that an ad states "Evenings" or just the abbreviation "Eves" will be disappointed, as will the applicant who overlooks a line saying "Some evenings and weekends reqd." Applicants overlooking information like "Apply in person" may email or mail their resumes and receive no response. The job hopeful with no previous experience and one reference must attend to information like "Minimum 5 yrs. exp, 3 refs," meaning they likely will not qualify.

## Employment Ads

Job applicants should pay attention to the information included in classified **employment ads**. On one hand, they do need to believe and accept certain statements, such as "Please, no phone calls," which is frequently used by employers posting ads on Craigslist and similar websites. New applicants just graduated from or still in college will be glad to see "No exp necessary" in some ads, indicating they need no previous work experience in that job category. "FT/PT" means the employer offers the options of working full-time or part-time, another plus for students. On the other hand, ad readers should also take into consideration the fact that many employers list all the attributes of their *ideal* employee, but they do not necessarily expect to find such a candidate. If a potential applicant's education, training, credentials, and experience are not exactly the same as what the employer lists as desired but are not radically different either, it can be productive to apply anyway, while honestly representing one's actual qualifications.

## Atlases

A **road atlas** is a publication designed to assist travelers who are driving on road trips rather than taking airplanes, trains, ships, etc. Travelers use road atlases to determine the following:

- Which routes to take and places to stop
- How to navigate specific cities
- How to locate landmarks
- How to estimate mileages and travel times
- View photographs of places they plan to visit
- Find other travel-related information

One familiar, reputable road atlas is published by the National Geographic Society. It includes the following:

- Maps of the United States, Canada, and Mexico
- Historic sites
- Scenic routes
- Recreation information
- Points of interest

Its Adventure Edition spotlights 100 top U.S. adventure destinations and most popular national parks. The best-selling road atlas in the United States, also probably the best-known and most trusted, is published annually by Rand McNally, which has published road atlases for many years. It includes maps, mileage charts, information on tourism and road construction, maps of individual city details, and the editor's favorite road trips (in the 2016 edition) including recommended points of interest en route.

## Owners' Manuals

An **owner's manual** is typically a booklet, but may also be as short as a page or as long as a book, depending on the individual instance. The purpose of an owner's manual is to give the owner instructions, usually step-by-step, for how to use a specific product. Manuals accompany consumer products as diverse as cars, computers, tablets, smartphones, printers, home appliances, shop machines, and many others. In addition to directions for operating products, they include important warnings of things *not* to do that pose safety or health hazards or can damage the product and void the manufacturer's product warranty, like immersion in water, exposure to high temperatures, operating something for too long, dropping fragile items, or rough handling. Manuals teach correct operating practices, sequences, precautions, and cautions, averting many costly and/or dangerous mishaps.

## Food Labels

When reading the **labels on food products**, it is often necessary to interpret the nutrition facts and other product information. Without the consumer's being aware and informed of this, much of this information can be very misleading. For example, a popular brand name of corn chips lists the calories, fat, etc. per serving in the nutrition facts printed on the bag, but on closer inspection, it defines a serving size as six chips—far fewer than most people would consume at a time. Serving sizes and the number of servings per container can be unrealistic. For example, a jumbo muffin's wrapper indicates it contains three servings. Not only do most consumers not divide a muffin and eat only part; but it is moreover rather difficult to cut a muffin into equal thirds. A king-sized package of chili cheese-flavored corn chips says it contains 4.5 servings per container. This is not very useful information, since people cannot divide the package into equal servings and are unlikely to eat four servings and then ½ a serving.

## Product Packaging

Consumers today cannot take **product labels** at face value. While many people do not read or even look at the information on packages before eating their contents, those who do must use more consideration and analysis than they might expect to understand it. For example, a well-known brand of strawberry-flavored breakfast toaster pastry displays a picture of four whole strawberries on the wrapper. While this looks appealing, encouraging consumers to infer the product contains wholesome fruit—and perhaps even believe it contains four whole strawberries—reading the ingredients list reveals it contains only 2 percent or less of dried strawberries. A consumer must be detail-oriented (and curious or motivated enough) to read the full ingredients list, which also reveals unhealthy corn syrup and high fructose corn syrup high on the list after enriched flour. Consumers must also educate themselves about euphemistically misleading terms: "enriched" flour has vitamins and minerals added, but it is refined flour without whole grain, bran, or fiber.

While manufacturers generally provide extensive information printed on their package labels, it is typically in very small print—many consumers do not read it—and even consumers who do read all the information must look for small details to discover that the information is often not realistic. For example, a box of brownie mix lists grams of fat, total calories, and calories from fat. However, by paying attention to small details like asterisks next to this information, and finding the additional information referenced by the asterisks, the consumer discovers that these amounts are for only the dry mix—not the added eggs, oil, or milk. Consumers typically do not eat dry cake mixes, and having to determine and add the fat and calories from the additional ingredients is inconvenient. In another example, a box of macaroni and cheese mix has an asterisk by the fat grams indicating these are for the macaroni only without the cheese, butter, or milk required, which contributes 6.4 times more fat.

Consumers can realize the importance of reading ***ingredient lists*** through an analogy: What might occur if they were to read only part of the directions on a standardized test? Reading only part of the directions on medications can have similar, even more serious consequences. Prescription drug packages typically contain inserts, which provide extremely extensive, thorough, detailed information, including results of clinical trials and statistics showing patient responses and adverse effects. Some over-the-counter medications include inserts, and some do not. "Active ingredients" are those ingredients making medication effective. "Inactive ingredients" including flavorings, preservatives, stabilizers, and emulsifiers have purposes, but not to treat symptoms. "Uses" indicates which symptoms a medication is meant to treat. "Directions" tell the dosage, frequency, maximum daily amount, and other requirements, like "Take with food," "Do not operate heavy machinery while using," etc. Drug labels also state how to store the product, like at what temperature or away from direct sunlight or humidity.

Many drugs which were previously available only by doctor prescription have recently become available over the counter without a prescription. While enough years of testing may have determined that these substances typically do not cause serious problems, consumers must nevertheless thoroughly read and understand all the information on the labels before taking them. If they do not, they could still suffer serious harm. For example, some individuals have allergies to specific substances. Both prescription and over-the-counter medication products list their ingredients, including warnings about allergies. Allergic reactions can include anaphylactic shock, which can be fatal if not treated immediately. Also, consumers must read and follow dosing directions: taking more than directed can cause harm, and taking less can be ineffective to treat symptoms. Some medication labels warn not to mix them with certain other drugs to avoid harmful drug interactions. Additionally, without reading ingredients, some consumers take multiple products including the same active ingredients, resulting in overdoses.

**Identifying Information from a Graphic Representation of Information**

*Line Graphs*

***Line graphs*** are useful for visually representing data that vary continuously over time, like an individual student's test scores. The horizontal or x-axis shows dates/times; the vertical or y-axis shows point values. A dot is plotted on the point where each horizontal date line intersects each vertical number line, and then these dots are connected, forming a line. Line graphs show whether changes in values over time exhibit trends like ascending, descending, flat, or more variable, like going up and down at different times. For example, suppose a student's scores on the same type of reading test were 75% in October, 80% in November, 78% in December, 82% in January, 85% in February, 88% in March, and 90% in April.

A line graph of these scores would look like this.

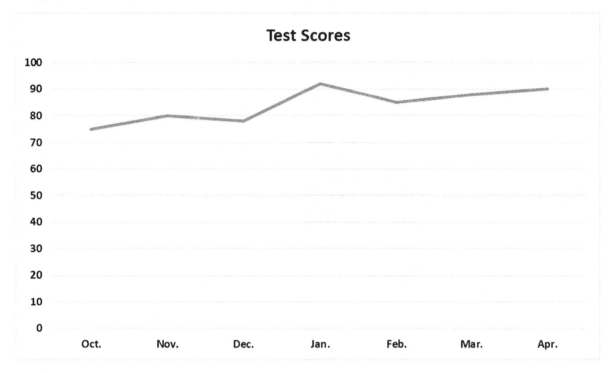

### Bar Graphs

**Bar graphs** feature equally spaced, horizontal or vertical rectangular bars representing numerical values. They can show change over time as line graphs do, but unlike line graphs, bar graphs can also show differences and similarities among values at a single point in time. Bar graphs are also helpful for visually representing data from different categories, especially when the horizontal axis displays some value that is not numerical, like basketball players with their heights:

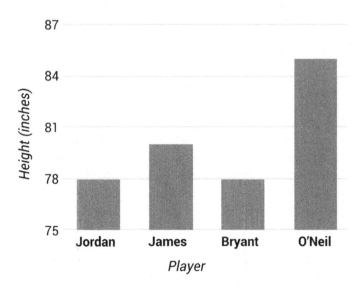

## Pie Charts

**Pie charts**, also called circle graphs, are good for representing percentages or proportions of a whole quantity because they represent the whole as a circle or "pie," with the various proportion values shown as "slices" or wedges of the pie. This gives viewers a clear idea of how much of a total each item occupies. For example, biologists may have information that 62% of dogs have brown eyes, 20% have green eyes, and 18% have blue eyes. A pie chart of these distributions would look like this:

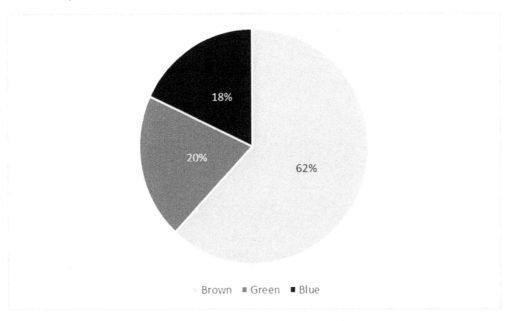

Brown ■ Green ■ Blue

## Pictograms

Magazines, newspapers, and other similar publications designed for consumption by the general public often use pictograms to represent data. **Pictograms** feature icons or symbols that look like whatever category of data is being counted, like little silhouettes shaped like human beings commonly used to represent people. If the data involve large numbers, like populations, one person symbol might represent one million people, or one thousand, etc. For smaller values, such as how many individuals out of ten fit a given description, one symbol might equal one person. Male and female silhouettes are used to differentiate gender, and child shapes for children. Little clock symbols are used to represent amounts of time, such as a given number of hours; calendar pages might depict months; suns and moons could show days and nights; hourglasses might represent minutes. While pictogram symbols are easily recognizable and appealing to general viewers, one disadvantage is that it is difficult to display partial symbols for in-between quantities.

## Recognizing Events in a Sequence

**Sequence structure** is the order of events in which a story or information is presented to the audience. Sometimes the text will be presented in chronological order, or sometimes it will be presented by displaying the most recent information first, then moving backwards in time. The sequence structure depends on the author, the context, and the audience. The structure of a text also depends on the genre in which the text is written. Is it literary fiction? Is it a magazine article? Is it instructions for how to complete a certain task? Different genres will have different purposes for switching up the sequence.

## Narrative Structure

The structure presented in literary fiction, called **narrative structure**, is the foundation on which the text moves. The narrative structure comes from the plot and setting. The plot is the sequence of events in the narrative that move the text forward through cause and effect. The setting is the place or time period in which the story takes place. Narrative structure has two main categories: linear and nonlinear.

*Linear Narrative*

A narrative is linear when it is told in chronological order. Traditional linear narratives will follow the plot diagram below depicting the narrative arc. The narrative arc consists of the exposition, conflict, rising action, climax, falling action, and resolution.

- **Exposition**: The exposition is in the beginning of a narrative and introduces the characters, setting, and background information of the story. The exposition provides the context for the upcoming narrative. Exposition literally means "a showing forth" in Latin.

- **Conflict**: In a traditional narrative, the conflict appears toward the beginning of the story after the audience becomes familiar with the characters and setting. The conflict is a single instance between characters, nature, or the self, in which the central character is forced to make a decision or move forward with some kind of action. The conflict presents something for the main character, or protagonist, to overcome.

- **Rising Action**: The rising action is the part of the story that leads into the climax. The rising action will develop the characters and plot while creating tension and suspense that eventually lead to the climax.

- **Climax**: The climax is the part of the story where the tension produced in the rising action comes to a culmination. The climax is the peak of the story. In a traditional structure, everything before the climax builds up to it, and everything after the climax falls from it. It is the height of the narrative, and it is usually either the most exciting part of the story or a turning point in the character's journey.

- **Falling action**: The falling action happens as a result of the climax. Characters continue to develop, although there is a wrapping up of loose ends here. The falling action leads to the resolution.

- **Resolution**: The resolution is where the story comes to an end and usually leaves the reader with the satisfaction of knowing what happened within the story and why. However, stories do not always end in this fashion. Sometimes readers can be confused or frustrated at the end from lack of information or the absence of a happy ending.

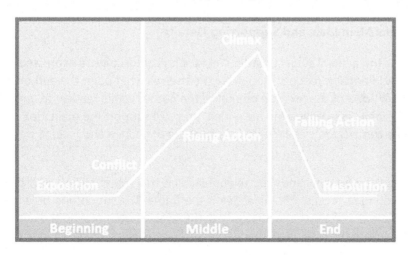

*Nonlinear Narrative*

A ***nonlinear narrative*** deviates from the traditional narrative because it does not always follow the traditional plot structure of the narrative arc. Nonlinear narratives may include structures that are disjointed, circular, or disruptive, in the sense that they do not follow chronological order. ***In medias res*** is an example of a nonlinear structure. *In medias res* is Latin for "in the middle of things," which is how many ancient texts, especially epic poems, began their story, such as Homer's *Iliad*. Instead of having a clear exposition with a full development of characters, they would begin right in the middle of the action.

Many modernist texts in the late nineteenth and early twentieth centuries experimented with disjointed narratives, moving away from traditional linear narrative. Disjointed narratives are depicted in novels like *Catch 22*, where the author, Joseph Heller, structures the narrative based on free association of ideas rather than chronology. Another nonlinear narrative can be seen in the novel *Wuthering Heights*, written by Emily Brontë; after the first chapter, the narrative progresses retrospectively instead of chronologically. There seem to be two narratives in *Wuthering Heights* working at the same time: a present narrative as well as a past narrative. Authors employ disrupting narratives for various reasons; some use it for the purpose of creating situational irony for the readers, while some use it to create a certain effect, such as excitement, discomfort, or fear.

*Sequence Structure in Technical Documents*

The purpose of technical documents, such as instructions manuals, cookbooks, or "user-friendly" documents, is to provide information to users as clearly and efficiently as possible. In order to do this, the sequence structure in technical documents should be as straightforward as possible. This usually involves some kind of chronological order or a direct sequence of events. For example, someone who is reading an instruction manual on how to set up their Smart TV wants directions in a clear, simple, straightforward manner that does not confuse them or leave them guessing about the proper sequence.

*Sequence Structure in Informational Texts*

The structure of informational texts depends on the specific genre. For example, a newspaper article may start by stating an exciting event that happened, then talk about that event in chronological order. Many informational texts also use cause and effect structure, which describes an event and then identifies reasons for why that event occurred. Some essays may write about their subjects by way of comparison and contrast, which is a structure that compares two things or contrasts them to highlight their differences. Other documents, such as proposals, will have a problem to solution structure, where the document highlights some kind of problem and then offers a solution. Finally, some informational texts are written with lush details and description in order to captivate the audience, allowing them to visualize the information presented to them. This type of structure is known as descriptive.

## Identifying the Topic, Main Idea, and Supporting Details

The ***topic*** of a text is the general subject matter. Text topics can usually be expressed in one word, or a few words at most. Additionally, readers should ask themselves what point the author is trying to make. This point is the ***main idea*** of the text, the one thing the author wants readers to know concerning the topic. Once the author has established the main idea, they will support the main idea by supporting details. ***Supporting details*** are evidence that support the main idea and include personal testimonies, examples, or statistics.

One analogy for these components and their relationships is that a text is like a well-designed house. The topic is the roof, covering all rooms. The main idea is the frame. The supporting details are the various rooms. To identify the topic of a text, readers can ask themselves what or who the author is writing about in the paragraph. To locate the main idea, readers can ask themselves what one idea the author wants readers to know about the topic. To identify supporting details, readers can put the main idea into question form and ask "what does the author use to prove or explain their main idea?"

Let's look at an example. An author is writing an essay about the Amazon rainforest and trying to convince the audience that more funding should go into protecting the area from deforestation. The author makes the argument stronger by including evidence of the benefits of the rainforest: it provides habitats to a variety of species, it provides much of the earth's oxygen which in turn cleans the atmosphere, and it is the home to medicinal plants that may be the answer to some of the world's deadliest diseases.

Here is an outline of the essay looking at topic, main idea, and supporting details:

**Topic:** Amazon rainforest
**Main Idea:** The Amazon rainforest should receive more funding in order to protect it from deforestation.
**Supporting Details:**
     1. It provides habitats to a variety of species
     2. It provides much of the earth's oxygen which in turn cleans the atmosphere
     3. It is home to medicinal plants that may be the answer to some of the world's deadliest diseases.

Notice that the topic of the essay is listed in a few key words: "Amazon rainforest." The main idea tells us what about the topic is important: that the topic should be funded in order to prevent deforestation. Finally, the supporting details are what author relies on to convince the audience to act or to believe in the truth of the main idea.

## Evaluating an Argument and its Specific Claims

When authors write text for the purpose of persuading others to agree with them, they assume a position with the subject matter about which they are writing. Rather than presenting information objectively, the author treats the subject matter subjectively so that the information presented supports his or her position. In their argumentation, the author presents information that refutes or weakens opposing positions. Another technique authors use in persuasive writing is to anticipate arguments against the position. When students learn to read subjectively, they gain experience with the concept of persuasion in writing, and learn to identify positions taken by authors. This enhances their reading comprehension and develops their skills for identifying pro and con arguments and biases.

There are five main parts of the classical argument that writers employ in a well-designed stance:

- Introduction: In the introduction to a classical argument, the author establishes goodwill and rapport with the reading audience, warms up the readers, and states the thesis or general theme of the argument.

- Narration: In the narration portion, the author gives a summary of pertinent background information, informs the readers of anything they need to know regarding the circumstances and environment surrounding and/or stimulating the argument, and establishes what is at risk or the stakes in the issue or topic. Literature reviews are common examples of narrations in academic writing.

- Confirmation: The confirmation states all claims supporting the thesis and furnishes evidence for each claim, arranging this material in logical order—e.g. from most obvious to most subtle or strongest to weakest.

- Refutation and Concession: The refutation and concession discuss opposing views and anticipate reader objections without weakening the thesis, yet permitting as many oppositions as possible.

- Summation: The summation strengthens the argument while summarizing it, supplying a strong conclusion and showing readers the superiority of the author's solution.

*Introduction*

A classical argument's ***introduction*** must pique reader interest, get readers to perceive the author as a writer, and establish the author's position. Shocking statistics, new ways of restating issues, or quotations or anecdotes focusing the text can pique reader interest. Personal statements, parallel instances, or analogies can also begin introductions—so can bold thesis statements if the author believes readers will agree. Word choice is also important for establishing author image with readers.

The introduction should typically narrow down to a clear, sound thesis statement. If readers cannot locate one sentence in the introduction explicitly stating the writer's position or the point they support, the writer probably has not refined the introduction sufficiently.

*Narration and Confirmation*

The ***narration*** part of a classical argument should create a context for the argument by explaining the issue to which the argument is responding, and by supplying any background information that influences the issue. Readers should understand the issues, alternatives, and stakes in the argument by the end of the narration to enable them to evaluate the author's claims equitably. The ***confirmation*** part of the classical argument enables the author to explain why they believe in the argument's thesis. The author builds a chain of reasoning by developing several individual supporting claims and explaining why that evidence supports each claim and also supports the overall thesis of the argument.

*Refutation and Concession and Summation*

The classical argument is the model for argumentative/persuasive writing, so authors often use it to establish, promote, and defend their positions. In the ***refutation*** aspect of the refutation and concession part of the argument, authors disarm reader opposition by anticipating and answering their possible objections, persuading them to accept the author's viewpoint. In the ***concession*** aspect, authors can concede those opposing viewpoints with which they agree. This can avoid weakening the author's thesis while establishing reader respect and goodwill for the author: all refutation and no concession can antagonize readers who disagree with the author's position. In the conclusion part of the classical argument, a less skilled writer might simply summarize or restate the thesis and related claims; however, this does not provide the argument with either momentum or closure. More skilled authors revisit the issues and the narration part of the argument, reminding readers of what is at stake.

## Distinguishing Between Fact and Opinion, Biases, and Stereotypes

*Facts and Opinions*

A ***fact*** is a statement that is true empirically or an event that has actually occurred in reality, and can be proven or supported by evidence; it is generally objective. In contrast, an ***opinion*** is subjective, representing something that someone believes rather than something that exists in the absolute. People's individual understandings, feelings, and perspectives contribute to variations in opinion. Though facts are typically objective in nature, in some instances, a statement of fact may be both factual and yet also subjective. For example, emotions are individual subjective experiences. If an individual says that they feel happy or sad, the feeling is subjective, but the statement is factual; hence, it is a subjective fact. In contrast, if one person tells another that the other is feeling happy or sad—whether this is true or not—that is an assumption or an opinion.

### Biases

**Biases** usually occur when someone allows their personal preferences or ideologies to interfere with what should be an objective decision. In personal situations, someone is biased towards someone if they favor them in an unfair way. In academic writing, being biased in your sources means leaving out objective information that would turn the argument one way or the other. The evidence of bias in academic writing makes the text less credible, so be sure to present all viewpoints when writing, not just your own, so to avoid coming off as biased. Being objective when presenting information or dealing with people usually allows the person to gain more credibility.

### Stereotypes

**Stereotypes** are preconceived notions that place a particular rule or characteristics on an entire group of people. Stereotypes are usually offensive to the group they refer to or allies of that group, and often have negative connotations. The reinforcement of stereotypes isn't always obvious. Sometimes stereotypes can be very subtle and are still widely used in order for people to understand categories within the world. For example, saying that women are more emotional and intuitive than men is a stereotype, although this is still an assumption used by many in order to understand the differences between one another.

## How an Author's Word Choice Shapes Meaning, Style, and Tone

Words can be very powerful. When written words are used with the intent to make an argument or support a position, the words used—and the way in which they are arranged—can have a dramatic effect on the readers. Clichés, colloquialisms, run-on sentences, and misused words are all examples of ways that word choice can negatively affect writing quality. Unless the writer carefully considers word choice, a written work stands to lose credibility.

If a writer's overall intent is to provide a clear meaning on a subject, he or she must consider not only the exact words to use, but also their placement, repetition, and suitability. Academic writing should be intentional and clear, and it should be devoid of awkward or vague descriptions that can easily lead to misunderstandings. When readers find themselves reading and rereading just to gain a clear understanding of the writer's intent, there may be an issue with word choice. Although the words used in academic writing are different from those used in a casual conversation, they shouldn't necessarily be overly academic either. It may be relevant to employ key words that are associated with the subject, but struggling to inject these words into a paper just to sound academic may defeat the purpose. If the message cannot be clearly understood the first time, word choice may be the culprit.

Word choice also conveys the author's attitude and sets a tone. Although each word in a sentence carries a specific **denotation**, it might also carry positive or negative **connotation**—and it is the connotations that set the tone and convey the author's attitude. Consider the following similar sentences:

It was the same old routine that happens every Saturday morning—eat, exercise, chores.

The Saturday morning routine went off without a hitch—eat, exercise, chores.

The first sentence carries a negative connotation with the author's "same old routine" word choice. The feelings and attitudes associated with this phrase suggest that the author is bored or annoyed at the

Saturday morning routine. Although the second sentence carries the same topic—explaining the Saturday morning routine—the choice to use the expression "without a hitch" conveys a positive or cheery attitude.

An author's writing style can likewise be greatly affected by word choice. When writing for an academic audience, for example, it is necessary for the author to consider how to convey the message by carefully considering word choice. If the author interchanges between third-person formal writing and second-person informal writing, the author's writing quality and credibility are at risk. Formal writing involves complex sentences, an objective viewpoint, and the use of full words as opposed to the use of a subjective viewpoint, contractions, and first- or second-person usage commonly found in informal writing.

Content validity, the author's ability to support the argument, and the audience's ability to comprehend the written work are all affected by the author's word choice.

**Evaluating the Author's Purpose in a Given Text**

Authors may have many purposes for writing a specific text. The ***author's purpose*** may be to try and convince readers to agree with their position on a subject, to impart information, or to entertain. Other writers are motivated to write from a desire to express their own feelings. Authors' purposes are their reasons for writing something. A single author may have one overriding purpose for writing or multiple reasons. An author may explicitly state their intention in the text, or the reader may need to infer that intention. When readers can identify the author's purpose, they are better able to analyze information in the text. By knowing why the author wrote the text, readers can glean ideas for how to approach it.

The following is a list of questions readers can ask in order to discern an author's purpose for writing a text:

- Does the title of the text give you any clues about its purpose?
- Was the purpose of the text to give information to readers?
- Did the author want to describe an event, issue, or individual?
- Was it written to express emotions and thoughts?
- Did the author want to convince readers to consider a particular issue?
- Do you think the author's primary purpose was to entertain?
- Why do you think the author wrote this text from a certain point of view?
- What is your response to the text as a reader?
- Did the author state their purpose for writing it?

Rather than simply consuming the text, readers should attempt to interpret the information being presented. Being able to identify an author's purpose efficiently improves reading comprehension, develops critical thinking, and makes students more likely to consider issues in depth before accepting writer viewpoints. Authors of fiction frequently write to entertain readers. Another purpose for writing fiction is making a political statement; for example, Jonathan Swift wrote "A Modest Proposal" (1729) as a political satire. Another purpose for writing fiction as well as nonfiction is to persuade readers to take some action or further a particular cause. Fiction authors and poets both frequently write to evoke certain moods; for example, Edgar Allan Poe wrote novels, short stories, and poems that evoke moods of gloom, guilt, terror, and dread. Another purpose of poets is evoking certain emotions: love is popular, as in Shakespeare's sonnets and numerous others. In "The Waste Land" (1922), T.S. Eliot evokes society's alienation, disaffection, sterility, and fragmentation.

Authors seldom directly state their purposes in texts. Some students may be confronted with nonfiction texts such as biographies, histories, magazine and newspaper articles, and instruction manuals, among others. To identify the purpose in nonfiction texts, students can ask the following questions:

- Is the author trying to teach something?
- Is the author trying to persuade the reader?
- Is the author imparting factual information only?
- Is this a reliable source?
- Does the author have some kind of hidden agenda?

To apply author purpose in nonfictional passages, students can also analyze sentence structure, word choice, and transitions to answer the aforementioned questions and to make inferences. For example, authors wanting to convince readers to view a topic negatively often choose words with negative connotations.

## Narrative Writing

**Narrative writing** tells a story. The most prominent type of narrative writing is the fictional novel. Here are some examples:

- Mark Twain's *The Adventures of Tom Sawyer* and *The Adventures of Huckleberry Finn*
- Victor Hugo's *Les Misérables*
- Charles Dickens' *Great Expectations, David Copperfield,* and *A Tale of Two Cities*
- Jane Austen's *Northanger Abbey, Mansfield Park, Pride and Prejudice, Sense and Sensibility,* and *Emma*
- Toni Morrison's *Beloved, The Bluest Eye*, and *Song of Solomon*
- Gabriel García Márquez's *One Hundred Years of Solitude* and *Love in the Time of Cholera*

Nonfiction works can also appear in narrative form. For example, some authors choose a narrative style to convey factual information about a topic, such as a specific animal, country, geographic region, and scientific or natural phenomenon.

Narrative writing tells a story, and the one telling the story is called the narrator. The narrator may be a fictional character telling the story from their own viewpoint. This narrator uses the first person (*I, me, my, mine* and *we, us, our,* and *ours*). The narrator may also be the author; for example, when Louisa May Alcott writes "Dear reader" in *Little Women,* she (the author) addresses us as readers. In this case, the novel is typically told in third person, referring to the characters as *he, she, they,* or *them.* Another more common technique is the omniscient narrator; in other words, the story is told by an unidentified individual who sees and knows everything about the events and characters—not only their externalized actions, but also their internalized feelings and thoughts. Second person narration, which addresses readers as you throughout the text, is more uncommon than the first and third person options.

## Expository Writing

**Expository writing** is also known as informational writing. Its purpose is not to tell a story as in narrative writing, to paint a picture as in descriptive writing, or to persuade readers to agree with something as in argumentative writing. Rather, its point is to communicate information to the reader. As such, the point of view of the author will necessarily be more objective. Expository writing does not appeal to emotions or reason, nor does it use subjective descriptions to sway the reader's opinion or thinking; rather, expository writing simply provides facts, evidence, observations, and objective descriptions of the subject matter. Some examples of expository writing include research reports, journal articles, books about history, academic textbooks, essays, how-to articles, user instruction manuals, news articles, and other factual journalistic reports.

## Technical Writing
**Technical writing** is similar to expository writing because it provides factual and objective information. Indeed, it may even be considered a subcategory of expository writing. However, technical writing differs from expository writing in two ways: (1) it is specific to a particular field, discipline, or subject, and (2) it uses technical terminology that belongs only to that area. Writing that uses technical terms is intended only for an audience familiar with those terms. An example of technical writing would be a manual on computer programming and use.

## Persuasive Writing
**Persuasive writing** or argumentative writing attempts to convince the reader to agree with the author's position. Some writers may respond to other writers' arguments by making reference to those authors or texts and then disagreeing with them. However, another common technique is for the author to anticipate opposing viewpoints, both from other authors and from readers. The author brings up these opposing viewpoints, and then refutes them before they can even be raised, strengthening the author's argument. Writers persuade readers by appealing to the readers' reason and emotion, as well as to their own character and credibility. Aristotle called these appeals **logos**, **pathos**, and **ethos**, respectively.

## Evaluating the Author's Point of View in a Given Text

When a writer tells a story using the first person, readers can identify this by the use of first-person pronouns, like *I, me, we, us,* etc. However, first-person narratives can be told by different people or from different points of view. For example, some authors write in the first person to tell the story from the main character's viewpoint, as Charles Dickens did in his novels *David Copperfield* and *Great Expectations*. Some authors write in the first person from the viewpoint of a fictional character in the story, but not necessarily the main character. For example, F. Scott Fitzgerald wrote *The Great Gatsby* as narrated by Nick Carraway, a character in the story, about the main characters, Jay Gatsby and Daisy Buchanan. Other authors write in the first person, but as the omniscient narrator—an often unnamed person who knows all of the characters' inner thoughts and feelings. Writing in first person as oneself is more common in nonfiction.

## Third Person
The **third-person** narrative is probably the most prevalent voice used in fictional literature. While some authors tell stories from the point of view and in the voice of a fictional character using the first person, it is a more common practice to describe the actions, thoughts, and feelings of fictional characters in the third person using *he, him, she, her, they, them,* etc.

Although plot and character development are both necessary and possible when writing narrative from a first-person point of view, they are also more difficult, particularly for new writers and those who find it unnatural or uncomfortable to write from that perspective. Therefore, writing experts advise beginning writers to start out writing in the third person. A big advantage of third-person narration is that the writer can describe the thoughts, feelings, and motivations of every character in a story, which is not possible for the first-person narrator. Third-person narrative can impart information to readers that the characters do not know. On the other hand, beginning writers often regard using the third-person point of view as more difficult because they must write about the feelings and thoughts of every character, rather than only about those of the protagonist.

## Second Person

Narrative written in the **second person** addresses someone else as "you." In novels and other fictional works, the second person is the narrative voice most seldom used. The primary reason for this is that it often reads in an awkward manner, which prevents readers from being drawn into the fictional world of the novel. The second person is more often used in informational text, especially in how-to manuals, guides, and other instructions.

## First Person

**First person** uses pronouns such as *I, me, we, my, us,* and *our.* Some writers naturally find it easier to tell stories from their own points of view, so writing in the first person offers advantages for them. The first-person voice is better for interpreting the world from a single viewpoint, and for enabling reader immersion in one protagonist's experiences. However, others find it difficult to use the first-person narrative voice. Its disadvantages can include overlooking the emotions of characters, forgetting to include description, producing stilted writing, using too many sentence structures involving "I did....", and not devoting enough attention to the story's "here-and-now" immediacy.

## Integrating Data from Multiple Sources in Various Formats, Including Media

### Books as Resources

When a student has an assignment to research and write a paper, one of the first steps after determining the topic is to select research sources. The student may begin by conducting an Internet or library search of the topic, may refer to a reading list provided by the instructor, or may use an annotated bibliography of works related to the topic. To evaluate the worth of the **book** for the research paper, the student first considers the book title to get an idea of its content. Then the student can scan the book's table of contents for chapter titles and topics to get further ideas of their applicability to the topic. The student may also turn to the end of the book to look for an alphabetized index. Most academic textbooks and scholarly works have these; students can look up key topic terms to see how many are included and how many pages are devoted to them.

### Journal Articles

Like books, **journal articles** are primary or secondary sources the student may need to use for researching any topic. To assess whether a journal article will be a useful source for a particular paper topic, a student can first get some idea about the content of the article by reading its title and subtitle, if any exists. Many journal articles, particularly scientific ones, include abstracts. These are brief summaries of the content. The student should read the abstract to get a more specific idea of whether the experiment, literature review, or other work documented is applicable to the paper topic. Students should also check the references at the end of the article, which today often contain links to related works for exploring the topic further.

### Encyclopedias and Dictionaries

**Dictionaries and encyclopedias** are both reference books for looking up information alphabetically. Dictionaries are more exclusively focused on vocabulary words. They include each word's correct spelling, pronunciation, variants, part(s) of speech, definitions of one or more meanings, and examples used in a sentence. Some dictionaries provide illustrations of certain words when these inform the meaning. Some dictionaries also offer synonyms, antonyms, and related words under a word's entry. Encyclopedias, like dictionaries, often provide word pronunciations and definitions. However, they have broader scopes: one can look up entire subjects in encyclopedias, not just words, and find comprehensive, detailed information about historical events, famous people, countries, disciplines of study, and many other things. Dictionaries are for finding word meanings, pronunciations, and spellings; encyclopedias are for finding breadth and depth of information on a variety of topics.

*Card Catalogs*

A **card catalog** is a means of organizing, classifying, and locating the large numbers of books found in libraries. Without being able to look up books in library card catalogs, it would be virtually impossible to find them on library shelves. Card catalogs may be on traditional paper cards filed in drawers, or electronic catalogs accessible online; some libraries combine both. Books are shelved by subject area; subjects are coded using formal classification systems—standardized sets of rules for identifying and labeling books by subject and author. These assign each book a call number: a code indicating the classification system, subject, author, and title. Call numbers also function as bookshelf "addresses" where books can be located. Most public libraries use the Dewey Decimal Classification System. Most university, college, and research libraries use the Library of Congress Classification. Nursing students will also encounter the National Institute of Health's National Library of Medicine Classification System, which major collections of health sciences publications utilize.

*Databases*

A **database** is a collection of digital information organized for easy access, updating, and management. Users can sort and search databases for information. One way of classifying databases is by content, i.e. full-text, numerical, bibliographical, or images. Another classification method used in computing is by organizational approach. The most common approach is a relational database, which is tabular and defines data so they can be accessed and reorganized in various ways. A distributed database can be reproduced or interspersed among different locations within a network.

An object-oriented database is organized to be aligned with object classes and subclasses defining the data. Databases usually collect files like product inventories, catalogs, customer profiles, sales transactions, student bodies, and resources. An associated set of application programs is a database management system or database manager. It enables users to specify which reports to generate, control access to reading and writing data, and analyze database usage. Structured Query Language (SQL) is a standard computer language for updating, querying, and otherwise interfacing with databases.

# Writing

**Elements of the Writing Process**

Skilled writers undergo a series of steps that comprise the writing process. The purpose of adhering to a structured approach to writing is to develop clear, meaningful, coherent work.

The stages are pre-writing/planning, organizing, drafting/writing, revising, and editing. Not every writer will necessarily follow all five stages for every project, but will judiciously employ the crucial components of the stages for most formal or important work. For example, a brief informal response to a short reading passage may not necessitate the need for significant organization after idea generation, but larger assignments and essays will likely mandate use of the full process.

*Pre-Writing/Planning*
*Brainstorming*
One of the most important steps in writing is pre-writing. Before drafting an essay or other assignment, it's helpful to think about the topic for a moment or two, in order to gain a more solid understanding of what the task is. Then, spend about five minutes jotting down the immediate ideas that could work for the essay. ***Brainstorming*** is a way to get some words on the page and offer a reference for ideas when drafting. Scratch paper is provided for writers to use any pre-writing techniques such as webbing, freewriting, or listing. Some writers prefer using graphic organizers during this phase. The goal is to get ideas out of the mind and onto the page.

*Freewriting*
Like brainstorming, ***freewriting*** is another prewriting activity to help the writer generate ideas. This method involves setting a timer for two or three minutes and writing down all ideas that come to mind about the topic using complete sentences. Once time is up, writers should review the sentences to see what observations have been made and how these ideas might translate into a more unified direction for the topic. Even if sentences lack sense as a whole, freewriting is an excellent way to get ideas onto the page in the very beginning stages of writing. Using complete sentences can make this a bit more challenging than brainstorming, but overall it is a worthwhile exercise, as it may force the writer to come up with more complete thoughts about the topic.

Once the ideas are on the page, it's time for the writer to turn them into a solid plan for the essay. The best ideas from the brainstorming results can then be developed into a more formal outline.

*Organizing*
Although sometimes it is difficult to get going on the brainstorming or prewriting phase, once ideas start flowing, writers often find that they have amassed too many thoughts that will not make for a cohesive and unified essay. During the ***organization*** stage, writers should examine the generated ideas, hone in on the important ones central to their main idea, and arrange the points in a logical and effective manner. Writers may also determine that some of the ideas generated in the planning process need further elaboration, potentially necessitating the need for research to gather information to fill the gaps.

Once a writer has chosen his or her thesis and main argument, selected the most applicable details and evidence, and eliminated the "clutter," it is time to strategically organize the ideas. This is often accomplished with an outline.

## Outlining

An **outline** is a system used to organize writing. When composing essays, outlining is important because it helps writers organize important information in a logical pattern using Roman numerals. Usually, outlines start out with the main ideas and then branch out into subgroups or subsidiary thoughts or subjects. Not only do outlines provide a visual tool for writers to reflect on how events, ideas, evidence, or other key parts of the argument relate to one another, but they can also lead writers to a stronger conclusion. The sample below demonstrates what a general outline looks like:

I. Introduction
  1. Background
  2. Thesis statement
II. Body
  1. Point A
     a. Supporting evidence
     b. Supporting evidence
  2. Point B
     a. Supporting evidence
     b. Supporting evidence
  3. Point C
     a. Supporting evidence
     b. Supporting evidence
III. Conclusion
  1. Restatement of main points.
  2. Memorable ending.

## Drafting/Writing

Now it comes time to actually write the essay. In this stage, writers should follow the outline they developed in the brainstorming process and try to incorporate the useful sentences penned in the freewriting exercise. The main goal of this phase is to put all the thoughts together in cohesive sentences and paragraphs.

It is helpful for writers to remember that their work here does not have to be perfect. This process is often referred to as **drafting** because writers are just creating a rough draft of their work. Because of this, writers should avoid getting bogged down on the small details.

## Referencing Sources

Anytime a writer quotes or paraphrases another text, they will need to include a citation. A **citation** is a short description of the work that a quote or information came from. The style manual your teacher wants you to follow will dictate exactly how to format that citation. For example, this is how one would cite a book according to the APA manual of style:

- *Format:* Last name, First initial, Middle initial. (Year Published) *Book Title.* City, State: Publisher.
- *Example:* Sampson, M. R. (1989). *Diaries from an alien invasion.* Springfield, IL: Campbell Press.

## Revising

**Revising** offers an opportunity for writers to polish things up. Putting one's self in the reader's shoes and focusing on what the essay actually says helps writers identify problems—it's a movement from the mindset of writer to the mindset of editor. The goal is to have a clean, clear copy of the essay.

The main goal of the revision phase is to improve the essay's flow, cohesiveness, readability, and focus. For example, an essay will make a less persuasive argument if the various pieces of evidence are scattered and presented illogically or clouded with unnecessary thought. Therefore, writers should consider their essay's structure and organization, ensuring that there are smooth transitions between sentences and paragraphs. There should be a discernable introduction and conclusion as well, as these crucial components of an essay provide readers with a blueprint to follow.

Additionally, if the writer includes copious details that do little to enhance the argument, they may actually distract readers from focusing on the main ideas and detract from the strength of their work. The ultimate goal is to retain the purpose or focus of the essay and provide a reader-friendly experience. Because of this, writers often need to delete parts of their essay to improve its flow and focus. Removing sentences, entire paragraphs, or large chunks of writing can be one of the toughest parts of the writing process because it is difficult to part with work one has done. However, ultimately, these types of cuts can significantly improve one's essay.

Lastly, writers should consider their voice and word choice. The voice should be consistent throughout and maintain a balance between an authoritative and warm style, to both inform and engage readers. One way to alter voice is through word choice. Writers should consider changing weak verbs to stronger ones and selecting more precise language in areas where wording is vague. In some cases, it is useful to modify sentence beginnings or to combine or split up sentences to provide a more varied sentence structure.

## Editing
Rather than focusing on content (as is the aim in the revising stage), the **editing** phase is all about the mechanics of the essay: the syntax, word choice, and grammar. This can be considered the proofreading stage. Successful editing is what sets apart a messy essay from a polished document.

The following areas should be considered when proofreading:

- Sentence fragments
- Awkward sentence structure
- Run-on sentences
- Incorrect word choice
- Grammatical agreement errors
- Spelling errors
- Punctuation errors
- Capitalization errors

One of the most effective ways of identifying grammatical errors, awkward phrases, or unclear sentences is to read the essay out loud. Listening to one's own work can help move the writer from simply the author to the reader.

During the editing phase, it's also important to ensure the essay follows the correct formatting and citation rules as dictated by the assignment.

## Recursive Writing Process
While the writing process may have specific steps, the good news is that the process is **recursive**, meaning the steps need not be completed in a particular order. Many writers find that they complete steps at the same time such as drafting and revising, where the writing and rearranging of ideas occur simultaneously or in very close order. Similarly, a writer may find that a particular section of a draft needs more development, and will go back to the prewriting stage to generate new ideas. The steps can be

repeated at any time, and the more these steps of the recursive writing process are employed, the better the final product will be.

*Practice Makes Prepared Writers*
Like any other useful skill, writing only improves with practice. While writing may come more easily to some than others, it is still a skill to be honed and improved. Regardless of a person's natural abilities, there is always room for growth in writing. Practicing the basic skills of writing can aid in preparations for the TEAS.

One way to build vocabulary and enhance exposure to the written word is through reading. This can be through reading books, but reading of any materials such as newspapers, magazines, and even social media count towards practice with the written word. This also helps to enhance critical reading and thinking skills, through analysis of the ideas and concepts read. Think of each new reading experience as a chance to sharpen these skills.

## Developing a Well-Organized Paragraph

A **paragraph** is a series of connected and related sentences addressing one topic. Writing good paragraphs benefits writers by helping them to stay on target while drafting and revising their work. It benefits readers by helping them to follow the writing more easily. Regardless of how brilliant their ideas may be, writers who do not present them in organized ways will fail to engage readers—and fail to accomplish their writing goals. A fundamental rule for paragraphing is to confine each paragraph to a single idea. When writers find themselves transitioning to a new idea, they should start a new paragraph. However, a paragraph can include several pieces of evidence supporting its single idea; and it can include several points if they are all related to the overall paragraph topic. When writers find each point becoming lengthy, they may choose instead to devote a separate paragraph to every point and elaborate upon each more fully.

An effective paragraph should have these elements:

- Unity: One major discussion point or focus should occupy the whole paragraph from beginning to end.

- Coherence: For readers to understand a paragraph, it must be coherent. Two components of coherence are logical and verbal bridges. In logical bridges, the writer may write consecutive sentences with parallel structure or carry an idea over across sentences. In verbal bridges, writers may repeat key words across sentences.

- A topic sentence: The paragraph should have a sentence that generally identifies the paragraph's thesis or main idea.

- Sufficient development: To develop a paragraph, writers can use the following techniques after stating their topic sentence:

  o Define terms
  o Cite data
  o Use illustrations, anecdotes, and examples
  o Evaluate causes and effects
  o Analyze the topic
  o Explain the topic using chronological order

A topic sentence identifies the main idea of the paragraph. Some are explicit, some implicit. The topic sentence can appear anywhere in the paragraph. However, many experts advise beginning writers to place each paragraph topic sentence at or near the beginning of its paragraph to ensure that their readers understand what the topic of each paragraph is. Even without having written an explicit topic sentence, the writer should still be able to summarize readily what subject matter each paragraph addresses. The writer must then fully develop the topic that is introduced or identified in the topic sentence. Depending on what the writer's purpose is, they may use different methods for developing each paragraph.

Two main steps in the process of organizing paragraphs and essays should both be completed after determining the writing's main point, while the writer is planning or outlining the work. The initial step is to give an order to the topics addressed in each paragraph. Writers must have logical reasons for putting one paragraph first, another second, etc. The second step is to sequence the sentences in each paragraph. As with the first step, writers must have logical reasons for the order of sentences. Sometimes the work's main point obviously indicates a specific order.

## Topic Sentences

To be effective, a topic sentence should be concise so that readers get its point without losing the meaning among too many words. As an example, in *Only Yesterday: An Informal History of the 1920s* (1931), author Frederick Lewis Allen's topic sentence introduces his paragraph describing the 1929 stock market crash: "The Bull Market was dead." This example illustrates the criteria of conciseness and brevity. It is also a strong sentence, expressed clearly and unambiguously. The topic sentence also introduces the paragraph, alerting the reader's attention to the main idea of the paragraph and the subject matter that follows the topic sentence.

Experts often recommend opening a paragraph with the topic sentences to enable the reader to realize the main point of the paragraph immediately. Application letters for jobs and university admissions also benefit from opening with topic sentences. However, positioning the topic sentence at the end of a paragraph is more logical when the paragraph identifies a number of specific details that accumulate evidence and then culminates with a generalization. While paragraphs with extremely obvious main ideas need no topic sentences, more often—and particularly for students learning to write—the topic sentence is the most important sentence in the paragraph. It not only communicates the main idea quickly to readers; it also helps writers produce and control information.

## Sentence Structures

## Incomplete Sentences

Four types of ***incomplete sentences*** are sentence fragments, run-on sentences, subject-verb and/or pronoun-antecedent disagreement, and non-parallel structure.

***Sentence fragments*** are caused by absent subjects, absent verbs, or dangling/uncompleted dependent clauses. Every sentence must have a subject and a verb to be complete. An example of a fragment is "Raining all night long," because there is no subject present. "It was raining all night long" is one correction. Another example of a sentence fragment is the second part in "Many scientists think in unusual ways. Einstein, for instance." The second phrase is a fragment because it has no verb. One correction is "Many scientists, like Einstein, think in unusual ways." Finally, look for "cliffhanger" words like *if, when, because,* or *although* that introduce dependent clauses, which cannot stand alone without an independent clause. For example, to correct the sentence fragment "If you get home early," add an independent clause: "If you get home early, we can go dancing."

## Run-On Sentences

A **run-on sentence** combines two or more complete sentences without punctuating them correctly or separating them. For example, a run-on sentence caused by a lack of punctuation is the following:

There is a malfunction in the computer system however there is nobody available right now who knows how to troubleshoot it.

One correction is, "There is a malfunction in the computer system; however, there is nobody available right now who knows how to troubleshoot it." Another is, "There is a malfunction in the computer system. However, there is nobody available right now who knows how to troubleshoot it."

An example of a comma splice of two sentences is the following:

Jim decided not to take the bus, he walked home.

Replacing the comma with a period or a semicolon corrects this. Commas that try and separate two independent clauses without a contraction are considered comma splices.

## Parallel Sentence Structures

**Parallel structure** in a sentence matches the forms of sentence components. Any sentence containing more than one description or phrase should keep them consistent in wording and form. Readers can easily follow writers' ideas when they are written in parallel structure, making it an important element of correct sentence construction. For example, this sentence lacks parallelism: "Our coach is a skilled manager, a clever strategist, and works hard." The first two phrases are parallel, but the third is not. Correction: "Our coach is a skilled manager, a clever strategist, and a hard worker." Now all three phrases match in form. Here is another example:

Fred intercepted the ball, escaped tacklers, and a touchdown was scored.

This is also non-parallel. Here is the sentence corrected:

Fred intercepted the ball, escaped tacklers, and scored a touchdown.

## Sentence Fluency

For fluent composition, writers must use a variety of sentence types and structures, and also ensure that they smoothly flow together when they are read. To accomplish this, they must first be able to identify fluent writing when they read it. This includes being able to distinguish among simple, compound, complex, and compound-complex sentences in text; to observe variations among sentence types, lengths, and beginnings; and to notice figurative language and understand how it augments sentence length and imparts musicality. Once students/writers recognize superior fluency, they should revise their own writing to be more readable and fluent. They must be able to apply acquired skills to revisions before being able to apply them to new drafts.

One strategy for revising writing to increase its **sentence fluency** is flipping sentences. This involves rearranging the word order in a sentence without deleting, changing, or adding any words. For example, the student or other writer who has written the sentence, "We went bicycling on Saturday" can revise it to, "On Saturday, we went bicycling." Another technique is using appositives. An **appositive** is a phrase or word that renames or identifies another adjacent word or phrase. Writers can revise for sentence fluency by inserting main phrases/words from one shorter sentence into another shorter sentence, combining them into one longer sentence, e.g. from "My cat Peanut is a gray and brown tabby. He loves hunting rats." to "My cat Peanut, a gray and brown tabby, loves hunting rats." Revisions can also connect shorter sentences by using conjunctions and commas and removing repeated words: "Scott likes eggs. Scott is allergic to eggs" becomes "Scott likes eggs, but he is allergic to them."

One technique for revising writing to increase sentence fluency is "padding" short, simple sentences by adding phrases that provide more details specifying why, how, when, and/or where something took place. For example, a writer might have these two simple sentences: "I went to the market. I purchased a cake." To revise these, the writer can add the following informative dependent and independent clauses and prepositional phrases, respectively: "Before my mother woke up, I sneaked out of the house and went to the supermarket. As a birthday surprise, I purchased a cake for her." When revising sentences to make them longer, writers must also punctuate them correctly to change them from simple sentences to compound, complex, or compound-complex sentences.

### Skills Writers Can Employ to Increase Fluency

One way writers can increase fluency is by varying the beginnings of sentences. Writers do this by starting most of their sentences with different words and phrases rather than monotonously repeating the same ones across multiple sentences. Another way writers can increase fluency is by varying the lengths of sentences. Since run-on sentences are incorrect, writers make sentences longer by also converting them from simple to compound, complex, and compound-complex sentences. The coordination and subordination involved in these also give the text more variation and interest, hence more fluency. Here are a few more ways writers can increase fluency:

- Varying the transitional language and conjunctions used makes sentences more fluent.
- Writing sentences with a variety of rhythms by using prepositional phrases.
- Varying sentence structure adds fluency.

## Use Grammar to Enhance Clarity in Writing

### Possessives

**Possessive forms** indicate possession, i.e. that something belongs to or is owned by someone or something. As such, the most common parts of speech to be used in possessive form are adjectives, nouns, and pronouns. The rule for correctly spelling/punctuating possessive nouns and proper nouns is with -'s, like "the woman's briefcase" or "Frank's hat." With possessive adjectives, however, apostrophes are not used: these include *my, your, his, her, its, our,* and *their,* like "my book," "your friend," "his car," "her house," "its contents," "our family," or "their property." Possessive pronouns include *mine, yours, his, hers, its, ours,* and *theirs.* These also have no apostrophes. The difference is that possessive adjectives take direct objects, whereas possessive pronouns replace them. For example, instead of using two possessive adjectives in a row, as in "I forgot my book, so Blanca let me use her book," which reads monotonously, replacing the second one with a possessive pronoun reads better: "I forgot my book, so Blanca let me use hers."

### Pronouns

There are three pronoun cases: subjective case, objective case, and possessive case. **Pronouns** as subjects are pronouns that replace the subject of the sentence, such as *I, you, he, she, it, we, they* and *who.* Pronouns as objects replace the object of the sentence, such as *me, you, him, her, it, us, them,* and *whom.* Pronouns that show possession are *mine, yours, hers, its, ours, theirs,* and *whose.* The following are examples of different pronoun cases:

- Subject pronoun: *She* ate the cake for her birthday. *I* saw the movie.
- Object pronoun: You gave *me* the card last weekend. She gave the picture to *him.*
- Possessive pronoun: That bracelet you found yesterday is *mine. His* name was Casey.

## Adjectives

**Adjectives** are descriptive words that modify nouns or pronouns. They may occur before or after the nouns or pronouns they modify in sentences. For example, in "This is a big house," *big* is an adjective modifying or describing the noun *house*. In "This house is big," the adjective is at the end of the sentence rather than preceding the noun it modifies.

A rule of punctuation that applies to adjectives is to separate a series of adjectives with commas. For example, "Their home was a large, rambling, old, white, two-story house." A comma should never separate the last adjective from the noun, though.

## Adverbs

Whereas adjectives modify and describe nouns or pronouns, **adverbs** modify and describe adjectives, verbs, or other adverbs. Adverbs can be thought of as answers to questions in that they describe when, where, how, how often, how much, or to what extent.

Many (but not all) adjectives can be converted to adverbs by adding *–ly*. For example, in "She is a quick learner," *quick* is an adjective modifying *learner*. In "She learns quickly," *quickly* is an adverb modifying *learns*. One exception is *fast*. *Fast* is an adjective in "She is a fast learner." However, *–ly* is never added to the word *fast*; it retains the same form as an adverb in "She learns fast."

## Verbs

A **verb** is a word or phrase that expresses action, feeling, or state of being. Verbs explain what their subject is *doing*. Three different types of verbs used in a sentence are action verbs, linking verbs, and helping verbs.

**Action verbs** show a physical or mental action. Some examples of action verbs are *play, type, jump, write, examine, study, invent, develop,* and *taste*. The following example uses an action verb:

> Kat *imagines* that she is a mermaid in the ocean.

The verb *imagines* explains what Kat is doing: she is imagining being a mermaid.

**Linking verbs** connect the subject to the predicate without expressing an action. The following sentence shows an example of a linking verb:

> The mango *tastes* sweet.

The verb *tastes* is a linking verb. The mango doesn't *do* the tasting, but the word *taste* links the mango to its predicate, sweet. Most linking verbs can also be used as action verbs, such as *smell, taste, look, seem, grow,* and *sound*. Saying something *is* something else is also an example of a linking verb. For example, if we were to say, "Peaches is a dog," the verb *is* would be a linking verb in this sentence, since it links the subject to its predicate.

**Helping verbs** are verbs that help the main verb in a sentence. Examples of helping verbs are *be, am, is, was, have, has, do, did, can, could, may, might, should,* and *must,* among others. The following are examples of helping verbs:

> Jessica *is* planning a trip to Hawaii.

> Brenda *does* not like camping.

> Xavier *should* go to the dance tonight.

Notice that after each of these helping verbs is the main verb of the sentence: *planning, like,* and *go.* Helping verbs usually show an aspect of time.

## Transitional Words and Phrases

In connected writing, some sentences naturally lead to others, whereas in other cases, a new sentence expresses a new idea. We use transitional phrases to connect sentences and the ideas they convey. This makes the writing coherent. Transitional language also guides the reader from one thought to the next. For example, when pointing out an objection to the previous idea, starting a sentence with "However," "But," or "On the other hand" is transitional. When adding another idea or detail, writers use "Also," "In addition," "Furthermore," "Further," "Moreover," "Not only," etc. Readers have difficulty perceiving connections between ideas without such transitional wording.

## Subject-Verb Agreement

Lack of **subject-verb agreement** is a very common grammatical error. One of the most common instances is when people use a series of nouns as a compound subject with a singular instead of a plural verb. Here is an example:

> Identifying the best books, locating the sellers with the lowest prices, and paying for them *is* difficult

instead of saying "*are* difficult." Additionally, when a sentence subject is compound, the verb is plural:

> He and his cousins *were* at the reunion.

However, if the conjunction connecting two or more singular nouns or pronouns is "or" or "nor," the verb must be singular to agree:

> That pen or another one like it is in the desk drawer.

If a compound subject includes both a singular noun and a plural one, and they are connected by "or" or "nor," the verb must agree with the subject closest to the verb: "Sally or her sisters go jogging daily"; but "Her sisters or Sally goes jogging daily."

Simply put, singular subjects require singular verbs and plural subjects require plural verbs. A common source of agreement errors is not identifying the sentence subject correctly. For example, people often write sentences incorrectly like, "The group of students *were* complaining about the test." The subject is not the plural "students" but the singular "group." Therefore, the correct sentence should read, "The group of students *was* complaining about the test." The converse also applies, for example, in this incorrect sentence: "The facts in that complicated court case *is* open to question." The subject of the sentence is not the singular "case" but the plural "facts." Hence the sentence would correctly be written: "The facts in that complicated court case *are* open to question." New writers should not be misled by the distance between the subject and verb, especially when another noun with a different number intervenes as in these examples. The verb must agree with the subject, not the noun closest to it.

## Pronoun-Antecedent Agreement

Pronouns within a sentence must refer specifically to one noun, known as the **antecedent**. Sometimes, if there are multiple nouns within a sentence, it may be difficult to ascertain which noun belongs to the pronoun. It's important that the pronouns always clearly reference the nouns in the sentence so as not to confuse the reader. Here's an example of an unclear pronoun reference:

> After Catherine cut Libby's hair, David bought her some lunch.

The pronoun in the examples above is *her*. The pronoun could either be referring to *Catherine* or *Libby*. Here are some ways to write the above sentence with a clear pronoun reference:

After Catherine cut Libby's hair, David bought Libby some lunch.

David bought Libby some lunch after Catherine cut Libby's hair.

But many times the pronoun will clearly refer to its antecedent, like the following:

After David cut Catherine's hair, he bought her some lunch.

**Conventions of Standard English Punctuation**

*Rules of Capitalization*

The first word of any document, and of each new sentence, is capitalized. Proper nouns, like names and adjectives derived from proper nouns, should also be capitalized. Here are some examples:

- Grand Canyon
- Pacific Palisades
- Golden Gate Bridge
- Freudian slip
- Shakespearian, Spenserian, or Petrarchan sonnet
- Irish song

Some exceptions are adjectives, originally derived from proper nouns, which through time and usage are no longer capitalized, like *quixotic, herculean*, or *draconian*. Capitals draw attention to specific instances of people, places, and things. Some categories that should be capitalized include the following:

- Brand names
- Companies
- Weekdays
- Months
- Governmental divisions or agencies
- Historical eras
- Major historical events
- Holidays
- Institutions
- Famous buildings
- Ships and other manmade constructions
- Natural and manmade landmarks
- Territories
- Nicknames
- Epithets
- Organizations
- Planets
- Nationalities
- Tribes
- Religions
- Names of religious deities

- Roads
- Special occasions, like the Cannes Film Festival or the Olympic Games

*Exceptions*

Related to American government, capitalize the noun Congress but not the related adjective congressional. Capitalize the noun U.S. Constitution, but not the related adjective constitutional. Many experts advise leaving the adjectives federal and state in lowercase, as in federal regulations or state water board, and only capitalizing these when they are parts of official titles or names, like Federal Communications Commission or State Water Resources Control Board. While the names of the other planets in the solar system are capitalized as names, Earth is more often capitalized only when being described specifically as a planet, like Earth's orbit, but lowercase otherwise since it is used not only as a proper noun but also to mean *land, ground, soil*, etc. While the name of the Bible should be capitalized, the adjective biblical should not. Regarding biblical subjects, the words heaven, hell, devil, and satanic should not be capitalized. Although race names like Caucasian, African-American, Navajo, Eskimo, East Indian, etc. are capitalized, white and black as races are not.

Names of animal species or breeds are not capitalized unless they include a proper noun. Then, only the proper noun is capitalized. Antelope, black bear, and yellow-bellied sapsucker are not capitalized. However, Bengal tiger, German shepherd, Australian shepherd, French poodle, and Russian blue cat are capitalized.

Other than planets, celestial bodies like the sun, moon, and stars are not capitalized. Medical conditions like tuberculosis or diabetes are lowercase; again, exceptions are proper nouns, like Epstein-Barr syndrome, Alzheimer's disease, and Down syndrome. Seasons and related terms like winter solstice or autumnal equinox are lowercase. Plants, including fruits and vegetables, like poinsettia, celery, or avocados, are not capitalized unless they include proper names, like Douglas fir, Jerusalem artichoke, Damson plums, or Golden Delicious apples.

*Titles and Names*

When official titles precede names, they should be capitalized, except when there is a comma between the title and name. But if a title follows or replaces a name, it should not be capitalized. For example, "the president" without a name is not capitalized, as in "The president addressed Congress." But with a name it is capitalized, like "President Obama addressed Congress." Or, "Chair of the Board Janet Yellen was appointed by President Obama." One exception is that some publishers and writers nevertheless capitalize President, Queen, Pope, etc., when these are not accompanied by names to show respect for these high offices. However, many writers in America object to this practice for violating democratic principles of equality. Occupations before full names are not capitalized, like owner Mark Cuban, director Martin Scorsese, or coach Roger McDowell.

Some universal rules for capitalization in composition titles include capitalizing the following:

- The first and last words of the title
- Forms of the verb *to be* and all other verbs
- Pronouns
- The word *not*

Universal rules for NOT capitalizing in titles include the articles *the, a,* or *an;* the conjunctions *and, or,* or *nor;* and the preposition *to,* or *to* as part of the infinitive form of a verb. The exception to all of these is UNLESS any of them is the first or last word in the title, in which case they are capitalized. Other words are subject to differences of opinion and differences among various stylebooks or methods. These include *as, but, if,* and *or,* which some capitalize and others do not. Some authorities say no preposition should ever be capitalized; some say prepositions five or more letters long should be capitalized. The *Associated Press Stylebook* advises capitalizing prepositions longer than three letters (like *about, across,* or *with*).

## Ellipses

**Ellipses** (. . .) signal omitted text when quoting. Some writers also use them to show a thought trailing off, but this should not be overused outside of dialogue. An example of an ellipses would be if someone is quoting a phrase out of a professional source but wants to omit part of the phrase that isn't needed: "Dr. Skim's analysis of pollen inside the body is clearly a myth . . . that speaks to the environmental guilt of our society."

## Commas

**Commas** separate words or phrases in a series of three or more. The Oxford comma is the last comma in a series. Many people omit this last comma, but many times it causes confusion. Here is an example:

> I love my sisters, the Queen of England and Madonna.

This example without the comma implies that the "Queen of England and Madonna" are the speaker's sisters. However, if the speaker was trying to say that they love their sisters, the Queen of England, as well as Madonna, there should be a comma after "Queen of England" to signify this.

Commas also separate two coordinate adjectives ("big, heavy dog") but not cumulative ones, which should be arranged in a particular order for them to make sense ("beautiful ancient ruins").

A comma ends the first of two independent clauses connected by conjunctions. Here is an example:

> I ate a bowl of tomato soup, and I was hungry very shortly after.

Here are some brief rules for commas:

- Commas follow introductory words like however, furthermore, well, why, and actually, among others.
- Commas go between city and state: Houston, Texas.
- If using a comma between a surname and Jr. or Sr. or a degree like M.D., also follow the whole name with a comma: "Martin Luther King, Jr., wrote that."
- A comma follows a dependent clause beginning a sentence: "Although she was very small, . . ."
- Nonessential modifying words/phrases/clauses are enclosed by commas: "Wendy, who is Peter's sister, closed the window."
- Commas introduce or interrupt direct quotations: "She said, 'I hate him.' 'Why,' I asked, 'do you hate him?'"

## Semicolons

**Semicolons** are used to connect two independent clauses but should never be used in the place of a comma. They can replace periods between two closely connected sentences: "Call back tomorrow; it can wait until then." When writing items in a series and one or more of them contains internal commas, separate them with semicolons, like the following:

> People came from Springfield, Illinois; Alamo, Tennessee; Moscow, Idaho; and other locations.

## Hyphens

Here are some rules concerning **hyphens**:

- Compound adjectives like state-of-the-art or off-campus are hyphenated.
- Original compound verbs and nouns are often hyphenated, like "throne-sat," "video-gamed," "no-meater."
- Adjectives ending in –ly are often hyphenated, like "family-owned" or "friendly-looking."
- "Five years old" is not hyphenated, but singular ages like "five-year-old" are.
- Hyphens can clarify. For example, in "stolen vehicle report," "stolen-vehicle report" clarifies that "stolen" modifies "vehicle," not "report."
- Compound numbers twenty-one through ninety-nine are spelled with hyphens.
- Prefixes before proper nouns/adjectives are hyphenated, like "mid-September" and "trans-Pacific."

## Parentheses

**Parentheses** enclose information such as an aside or more clarifying information: "She ultimately replied (after deliberating for an hour) that she was undecided." They are also used to insert short, in-text definitions or acronyms: "His FBS (fasting blood sugar) was higher than normal." When parenthetical information ends the sentence, the period follows the parentheses: "We received new funds ($25,000)." Only put periods within parentheses if the whole sentence is inside them: "Look at this. (You'll be astonished.)" However, this can also be acceptable as a clause: "Look at this (you'll be astonished)." Although parentheses appear to be part of the sentence subject, they are not, and do not change subject-verb agreement: "Will (and his dog) was there."

## Quotation Marks

**Quotation marks** are typically used when someone is quoting a direct word or phrase someone else writes or says. Additionally, quotation marks should be used for the titles of poems, short stories, songs, articles, chapters, and other shorter works. When quotations include punctuation, periods and commas should *always* be placed inside of the quotation marks.

When a quotation contains another quotation inside of it, the outer quotation should be enclosed in double quotation marks and the inner quotation should be enclosed in single quotation marks. For example: "Timmy was begging, 'Don't go! Don't leave!'" When using both double and single quotation marks, writers will find that many word-processing programs may automatically insert enough space between the single and double quotation marks to be visible for clearer reading. But if this is not the case, the writer should write/type them with enough space between to keep them from looking like three single quotation marks. Additionally, non-standard usages, terms used in an unusual fashion, and technical terms are often clarified by quotation marks. Here are some examples:

My "friend," Dr. Sims, has been micromanaging me again.

This way of extracting oil has been dubbed "fracking."

## Apostrophes

One use of the **apostrophe** is followed by an *s* to indicate possession, like *Mrs. White's home* or *our neighbor's dog*. When using the *'s* after names or nouns that also end in the letter *s*, no single rule applies: some experts advise adding both the apostrophe and the *s*, like "the Jones's house," while others prefer using only the apostrophe and omitting the additional *s*, like "the Jones' house." The wisest expert advice is to pick one formula or the other and then apply it consistently. Newspapers and magazines often use *'s* after common nouns ending with *s*, but add only the apostrophe after proper nouns or names ending with *s*. One common error is to place the apostrophe before a name's final *s* instead of after it: "Ms. Hasting's book" is incorrect if the name is Ms. Hastings.

Plural nouns should not include apostrophes (e.g. "apostrophe's"). Exceptions are to clarify atypical plurals, like verbs used as nouns: "These are the do's and don'ts." Irregular plurals that do not end in *s* always take apostrophe-*s*, not *s*-apostrophe—a common error, as in "childrens' toys," which should be "children's toys." Compound nouns like mother-in-law, when they are singular and possessive, are followed by apostrophe-*s*, like "your mother-in-law's coat." When a compound noun is plural and possessive, the plural is formed before the apostrophe-*s*, like "your sisters-in-laws' coats." When two people named possess the same thing, use apostrophe-*s* after the second name only, like "Dennis and Pam's house."

## Conventions of Standard English Spelling

### Homonyms, Homophones, and Homographs

**Homophones** are words that sound the same in speech but have different spellings and meanings. For example, *to, too,* and *two* all sound alike, but have three different spellings and meanings. Homophones with different spellings are also called **heterographs**. **Homographs** are words that are spelled identically but have different meanings. If they also have different pronunciations, they are **heteronyms**. For example, *tear* pronounced one way means a drop of liquid formed by the eye; pronounced another way, it means to rip. Homophones that are also homographs are **homonyms**. For example, *bark* can mean the outside of a tree or a dog's vocalization; both meanings have the same spelling. *Stalk* can mean a plant stem or to pursue and/or harass somebody; these are spelled and pronounced the same. *Rose* can mean a flower or the past tense of *rise*. Many non-linguists confuse things by using "homonym" to mean sets of words that are homophones but not homographs, and also those that are homographs but not homophones.

The word *row* can mean to use oars to propel a boat; a linear arrangement of objects or print; or an argument. It is pronounced the same with the first two meanings, but differently with the third. Because it is spelled identically regardless, all three meanings are homographs. However, the two meanings pronounced the same are homophones, whereas the one with the different pronunciation is a heteronym. By contrast, the word *read* means to peruse language, whereas the word *reed* refers to a marsh plant. Because these are pronounced the same way, they are homophones; because they are spelled differently, they are heterographs. Homonyms are both homophones and homographs—pronounced and spelled identically, but with different meanings. One distinction between homonyms is of those with separate, unrelated etymologies, called "true" homonyms, e.g. *skate* meaning a fish or *skate* meaning to glide over ice/water. Those with common origins are called polysemes or polysemous homonyms, e.g. the *mouth* of an animal/human or of a river.

### Irregular Plurals

While many words in English can become plural by adding –s or –es to the end, there are some words that have irregular plural forms. One type includes words that are spelled the same whether they are singular or plural, such as *deer, fish, salmon, trout, sheep, moose, offspring, species, aircraft, etc.* The spelling rule for making these words plural is simple: they do not change. Other irregular English plurals change form based on vowel shifts, linguistic mutations, or grammatical and spelling conventions from their languages of origin, like Latin or German. Some examples include *child* and *children; die* and *dice; foot* and *feet; goose* and *geese; louse* and *lice; man* and *men; mouse* and *mice; ox* and *oxen; person* and *people; tooth* and *teeth;* and *woman* and *women.*

## Contractions

**Contractions** are formed by joining two words together, omitting one or more letters from one of the component words, and replacing the omitted letter(s) with an apostrophe. An obvious yet often forgotten rule for spelling contractions is to place the apostrophe where the letters were omitted; for example, spelling errors like *did'nt* for *didn't. Didn't* is a contraction of *did not.* Therefore, the apostrophe replaces the "o" that is omitted from the "not" component. Another common error is confusing contractions with possessives because both include apostrophes, e.g. spelling the possessive *its* as "it's," which is a contraction of "it is"; spelling the possessive *their* as "they're," a contraction of "they are"; spelling the possessive *whose* as "who's," a contraction of "who is"; or spelling the possessive *your* as "you're," a contraction of "you are."

## Frequently Misspelled Words

One source of spelling errors is not knowing whether to drop the final letter *e* from a word when its form is changed by adding an ending to indicate the past tense or progressive participle of a verb, converting an adjective to an adverb, a noun to an adjective, etc. Some words retain the final *e* when another syllable is added; others lose it. For example, *true* becomes *truly; argue* becomes *arguing; come* becomes *coming; write* becomes *writing;* and *judge* becomes *judging.* In these examples, the final *e* is dropped before adding the ending. But *severe* becomes *severely; complete* becomes *completely; sincere* becomes *sincerely; argue* becomes *argued;* and *care* becomes *careful.* In these examples, the final *e* is retained before adding the ending. Note that some words, like *argue* in these examples, drops the final *e* when the *–ing* ending is added to indicate the participial form; but the regular past tense ending of *–ed* makes it *argued,* in effect replacing the final *e* so that *arguing* is spelled without an *e* but *argued* is spelled with one.

Other commonly misspelled English words are those containing the vowel combinations *ei* and *ie.* Many people confuse these two. Some examples of words with the *ei* combination include:

> *ceiling, conceive, leisure, receive, weird, their, either, foreign, sovereign, neither, neighbors, seize, forfeit, counterfeit, height, weight, protein,* and *freight*

Words with *ie* include *piece, believe, chief, field, friend, grief, relief, mischief, siege, niece, priest, fierce, pierce, achieve, retrieve, hygiene, science,* and *diesel.* A rule that also functions as a mnemonic device is "I before E except after C, or when sounded like A as in 'neighbor' or 'weigh'." However, it is obvious from the list above that many exceptions exist.

People often misspell certain words by confusing whether they have the vowel *a, e,* or *i.* For example, in the following correctly spelled words, the vowel in boldface is the one people typically get wrong by substituting one of the others for it:

> cem**e**tery, quant**i**ties, ben**e**fit, privi**l**ege, unpleas**a**nt, sep**a**rate, independ**e**nt, excell**e**nt, cat**e**gories, indispens**a**ble, and irrelev**a**nt

Some words with final syllables that sound the same when spoken but are spelled differently include *unpleasant, independent, excellent,* and *irrelevant.* Another source of misspelling is whether or not to double consonants when adding suffixes. For example, double the last consonant before *–ed* and *–ing* endings in *controlled, beginning, forgetting, admitted, occurred, referred,* and *hopping,* but do not double before the suffix in *shining, poured, sweating, loving, hating, smiling,* and *hoping.*

One final example of common misspellings involves either the failure to include silent letters or the converse of adding extraneous letters. If a letter is not pronounced in speech, it is easy to leave it out in writing. For example, some people omit the silent *u* in *guarantee*, overlook the first *r* in *surprise*, leave out the *z* in *realize*, fail to double the *m* in *recommend*, leave out the middle *i* from *aspirin*, and exclude the *p* from *temperature*. The converse error, adding extra letters, is common in words like *until* by adding a second *l* at the end; or by inserting a superfluous syllabic *a* or *e* in the middle of *athletic*, reproducing a common mispronunciation.

# Speaking

The Speaking section of the IELTS™ consists of an oral interview between the test taker and the administrator. This portion of the exam lasts 11–14 minutes, gets recorded, and measures the candidate's ability to effectively communicate in English. The Speaking section is the only section of the IELTS™ exam that can be taken on a separate day—up to a week before or after the administration of the rest of the exam. Test takers can consult with their planned testing center for further information and to schedule their Speaking section. There are three components to this test section, each of which are specifically designed to satisfy a specific purpose in terms of the required interaction pattern, task input, and anticipated output from the test taker. The three parts, which occur in the listed order, are as follows:

- **Introduction and interview**: This section lasts 4–5 minutes and begins with general introductions between the examiner and the test taker. The examiner will then ask the test taker basic questions about familiar life topics such as his or her family, home life, hobbies, and studies. Examiners read the questions from a script to ensure consistency in the testing experience between candidates.

- **Individual long turn**: The examiner will hand the test taker a card that contains a speaking topic prompt, and lists specific aspects of the topic that must be addressed in the response, with the added instruction that the test taker must explain at least one of the points in detail. After the test taker finishes delivering his or her response, the examiner will ask one or two additional questions related to the same topic. In total, this section lasts 3–4 minutes: one minute for the test taker to prepare after reading the card, 1–2 minutes for the oral response, and then approximately one minute for the follow-up questions. Test takers are encouraged to practice their time management skills and practice talking 90–120 seconds on one sustained topic. On the exam, answering all points on the prompt in much less than 90 seconds will typically result in score deductions due to fact that such a short answer is likely incomplete. However, it should be noted that even if test takers have not addressed all of tasks on the prompt or have not finished sharing their thoughts, the examiner will stop the test taker after two minutes. Given the narrow window within the time constraints, test takers should take full advantage of the one-minute preparation time to structure their speech within the confines of the time requirements. Test takers are permitted to jot down notes or put together a basic outline during the preparation period. This strategy can help ensure all salient points will be given ample time. Examiners usually expect test takers to draw upon some of their own life experiences when responding to long turn prompts. The response should use language appropriately and effectively, and be coherent and well-organized.

- **Discussion**: This section lasts 4–5 minutes and involves a back-and-forth conversation between the test takers and examiner about the same topic addressed in the individual long turn part. However, in the discussion section, the topic is examined in greater depth, or in a more abstract or global way. During this part of the exam, the examiner is looking for evidence of the test taker's ability to justify his or her opinion on an issue and analyze other potential viewpoints.

For each of the three Speaking section tasks just described, test takers are evaluated on the following four criteria:

- **Fluency and coherence**: Examiners evaluate the test taker's ability to speak fluidly, coherently, with a steady and natural rate, and with logically connected thoughts. Cohesive devices, such as conjunctions, connecting words, and pronouns, which work to effectively link words, phrases, sentences, and ideas should be used appropriately.

- **Lexical resource**: Test takers are evaluated on their vocabulary and word choices, particularly the range and precision of language used to accurately convey their intended meaning. Included within this criterion is the degree to which test takers can fluidly fill vocabulary gaps with other words in their working memory.

- **Grammatical range and accuracy:** Successful test takers speak with relatively few grammatical errors, and include sentences with varying lengths, complexities, and structures. The impact that errors impart on the communication meaning is also weighed.

- **Pronunciation:** Test takers are evaluated on their ability to deliver intelligible, easily-understood speech with proper pronunciation.

Although the Speaking section is often one of the more intimidating ones for test takers, it is relatively easy to prepare for because there are almost an infinite number of opportunities to practice before the exam. It is recommended that candidates capitalize on every opportunity to practice their English-speaking skills. Doing so will breed confidence and competence for the exam and for real life, where conversing in English will be required outside of testing situations. Shopping, finding study buddies, joining clubs or social organizations, talking with neighbors, or volunteering in the community, are among some of the many ways to accrue speaking practice time.

Besides taking advantage of every opportunity to practice English-speaking skills, successful test takers often implement the following strategies:

### Don't Prepare Memorized Answers

While it is important to practice speaking on a variety of topics, candidates should not prepare answers and then try to memorize them before test day. Even though there are certain topics that will likely be addressed (such as hobbies, studies, family life, etc.), pre-preparing an answer often lowers the test taker's score because it often causes a speaking pattern that sounds monotone, and is devoid of authenticity and feeling. Test takers who have memorized their answers also run the risk of not directly and exactly answering the question posed because they get caught up in adhering to the script they have practiced. They will try to force that similar question to stand-in for the one that was actually asked. Conversing requires spontaneity and the ability to adjust on the fly based on how the conversation partner responds.

### Time Yourself During Practice Sessions

Test takers should practice with a stopwatch to gain a sense of how long answers should be, and how much needs to be said to fill that time. This is especially important for the long turn, where it's critical to talk as close to two minutes—without exceeding it—as possible.

### To Elaborate, Answer the "Why"

Test takers often feel unsure of how to fill the speaking time or flesh out their answers, particularly in the first two parts of the Speaking section. Successful test takers elaborate and expand their answers by explaining the "why" behind them. For example, a common question in part one is, "What are your hobbies?" An unprepared test taker might respond, "I enjoy basketball, taking my nephew to the park, and riding my bike." However, this answer is brief and does not share much about the character and personality of the test taker. Instead, he or she could respond similarly, but explain why those activities are personally enjoyable. For example, "I enjoy basketball, taking my nephew to the park, and riding my bike because I really like being active. I'm teaching my nephew to play basketball because he has trouble sitting still in class. It's been special to have activity to bond over in the past few months." With that said, it is important to stay on topic. Answering the "why" is helpful and appropriate, but test takers should not veer too far off the original prompt.

## Record Yourself

Many test takers feel anxious or self-conscious with the presence of the recording machine during the test. An easy way to eliminate the stress caused by the awareness of the recorder is for test takers to practice recording themselves at home. Reviewing recordings is an excellent study strategy. Test takers can listen to their grammar, vocabulary, cohesiveness, coherence, and "accent." Examiners appreciate when test takers attempt to speak naturally, with varied tone and pitch; test takers can practice and verify this quality of their speech by reviewing self-recordings.

## Aim for Fluency Over Vocabulary

A common misconception among test takers regarding the Speaking section is that using advanced vocabulary, and a very wide range of words, is the key to obtaining a high score and demonstrating mastery of conversing in English. However, examiners are typically more impressed when test takers speak fluidly, and move along at a natural pace, without inserting frequent pauses to search for the "perfect" or showy vocabulary word. Some pauses are normal and to be expected, but it is generally advisable for test takers to prioritize delivering a smooth, fluent, and fluid speech over stilted sentences with too many breaks that keep interrupting the flow. Test takers should select the first word that comes to mind that fits appropriately in the gap when pausing to recall a workable word.

## Don't Be Afraid to Ask

It is normal for test takers to feel nervous and reluctant to ask the examiner for clarification or to repeat a question, but it's perfectly acceptable for them to do so. Even in normal conversations—outside of testing scenarios—people ask for clarification before answering questions. On test day, when in doubt, it's better for test takers to double-check with the examiner to confirm they understand what is being asked before delivering a long, drawn-out answer to a question that was misunderstood. However, test takers should be careful to not abuse this advice and ask the examiner to repeat or define lots of words.

## Share Yourself

Where possible, it is also advantageous for candidates to share their personal experiences and tell stories from their lives during the exam. This is particularly useful during the discussion part because it conveys a level of trust and comfort with the examiner. It also makes for a more captivating, unique conversation. Speakers who pull from their own experiences and share their true thoughts and feeling also tend to speak more naturally, allowing for a more emotive, natural voice, and more robust answers, both which factor into improving one's score.

## Stay Calm and Speak with Authority

Mistakes will happen. Test takers who notice the mistake quickly can, and should, try to correct it if they know how, as this demonstrates an interest in learning and improving, and an awareness of the error. However, if the test taker is not sure how to correct the mistake or has realized the issue several sentences later, he or she should just keep moving on, staying as confident and self-assured as possible. Examiners understand that test takers are still learning and that mistakes will happen. Staying calm will help the test taker ensure that his or her focus is maintained, which can help prevent further mistakes.

Moreover, test takers should smile, present themselves with confidence, and speak loudly and with authority. Each test taker is unique and has his or her own life experiences, interests, and ideas to share. Test takers should be proud of what they bring to the world and feel confident in their ability to share meaningful answers to the examiner.

# General Training Test

## *Listening*

Directions: The Listening section measures your ability to understand conversations and lectures in English. In this test, you will listen to several pieces of content and answer questions after each one. The questions typically ask about the main idea and supporting details. Some questions ask about a speaker's purpose or attitude. Answer the questions based on what is stated or implied by the speakers.

Listen to all of these passages here:

**www.apexprep.com/ielts**

Note that on the actual test, you can take notes while you listen and use your notes to help you answer the questions. Your notes will not be scored.

For your convenience, the transcripts of all of the audio passages are provided after the answer explanations. However, on the actual test, no such transcripts will be provided.

### Passage #1: Employee Conversation

**Listen Here: www.apexprep.com/ielts**

1. What is the main focus of the discussion between the employee and employer?
    a. The employee's previous work experience
    b. A coworker's termination
    c. The employee's current workload
    d. Dinner plans

2. Why was Peter fired?
    a. He threatened coworkers with violence.
    b. He invited the employee to dinner.
    c. He spent too much time at the employee's desk.
    d. He falsified reports of employees who refused his invitations.

3. Why was the employee surprised that Peter had been fired?
    a. The employee is in a romantic relationship with Peter.
    b. Peter is her direct supervisor.
    c. The employee experienced similar harassment at her previous jobs.
    d. Peter had previously been helpful to the employee.

4. What did the employee forget to tell the employer at first?
    a. Peter spends a lot of time at her desk.
    b. Peter once invited her to dinner.
    c. Peter has been very helpful.
    d. Peter tampered with her reports.

*Questions 5–10: Complete the sentences below with NO MORE THAN ONE WORD per answer.*

The employer ultimately had to 5. _____ Peter.

Several employees filed 6. _____ against Peter for harassment.

The employer discovered Peter's misbehavior after discovering he altered 7. _____

The employee reported that Peter had asked her to go to 8. _____ last week.

The employer first contacted the employee about this matter by 9. _____.

Peter spent a lot of time loitering around the employee's 10. _____.

## Passage #2: Court Decision

### Listen Here: www.apexprep.com/ielts

11. Which main issue did the court's decision address?
    a. Whether schools could apply the doctrine of "separate but equal"
    b. Whether schools should be concerned with their students' mental development
    c. Whether some races of people are inferior to others
    d. Whether the court has the power to change schools' policies

12. What did the court conclude?
    a. The doctrine of "separate but equal" is the same as segregation, which was already illegal.
    b. The doctrine of "separate but equal" harms children, and therefore it cannot be allowed to continue.
    c. The doctrine of "separate but equal" is beyond the court's power to change.
    d. The doctrine of "separate but equal" is risky, but it has a place in schools.

13. In the segregated schools at the center of this lawsuit, on what basis were schoolchildren separated?
    a. Race
    b. Educational achievement
    c. Mental development
    d. Psychological traits

14. How did segregation harm schoolchildren?
    a. Segregation meant the schoolchildren couldn't attend school regularly.
    b. Segregation forced the schoolchildren to attend schools outside their community.
    c. Segregation caused the schoolchildren to feel inferior and unmotivated.
    d. Segregation unfairly separated children based on age and qualifications.

*Questions 15–20: Complete the notes below with NO MORE THAN ONE WORD per answer.*

| Legal Decision Notes |
|---|
| Public (15) _____ prohibited (16) _____ schoolchildren from attending. |
| *Plessy v. Ferguson* created legal basis for racial (17) _____. |
| Black schoolchildren sue to overturn *Plessy*. |
| Court finds that the separation of races inherently creates a sense of (18) _____. |
| Racially (19) _____ system: better for all children. |
| Final decision: "Separate but (20) _____" is overturned. |

**Passage #3: Professor/Student Conversation**

**Listen Here: www.apexprep.com/ielts**

21. What is the main topic of this conversation?
    a. Academic writing
    b. Francisco Franco
    c. Advice on paper topics
    d. Grading philosophies

22. What does the professor believe is "critical for academic writing"?
    a. Asking for feedback
    b. A strong thesis statement
    c. Adequate research
    d. Run-on sentences

23. According to the professor, what should a thesis statement do?
    a. A thesis statement helps organize the paper, and it's always written in a neutral tone.
    b. A thesis statement conveys the paper's central message in one to two paragraphs.
    c. A thesis statement functions as the paper's introduction.
    d. A thesis statement clearly and concisely tells the reader what the paper is about.

24. Which of the following was NOT a problem with the thesis statement in the student's last paper?
    a. The thesis statement was a run-on sentence.
    b. The paper didn't follow the thesis.
    c. The thesis statement included evidence that the paper never mentioned again.
    d. The thesis statement contained spelling errors.

*Questions 25–27: Complete the table below with NO MORE THAN ONE WORD per answer.*

| Professor's Feedback | |
|---|---|
| **Issues** | **Improvement** |
| Unclear 25._____ | Clear and concise |
| Poor evidence | Relevant evidence |
| Run-on 26._____ | 27._____ message |

*Questions 28–30: Answer the questions below with NO MORE THAN TWO WORDS per answer.*

28. Which political ideology did the student choose to write about?

29. Along with her thesis, what does the student need to specifically improve to reach her potential?

30. If the student can't find enough sources for Francisco Franco, whom does she plan to write about?

**Passage #4: Lecture**

**Listen Here: www.apexprep.com/ielts**

31. What is the lecture's primary purpose?
   a. To advocate for a law prohibiting propaganda
   b. To explain the power of visual propaganda
   c. To express concern over terrorism and extremism
   d. To call for more studies to be conducted on propaganda

32. According to the professor, how do the early and more recent studies of propaganda differ from one another?
   a. The early studies didn't have a large enough sample size, and the more recent studies corrected this mistake.
   b. The early studies didn't account for the growth in propaganda online, especially in visual form, which is the main focus of the more recent studies.
   c. The early studies focused only on government-issued propaganda, and the more recent studies expanded the scope to cover non-state actors like terrorist groups.
   d. The early studies considered propaganda to be a top-down transaction, while the more recent studies believe it's a two-way transaction.

33. Why does the professor believe the "basis for the visual image" is biological and universal?
   a. All humans process information visually, which is itself a biological function.
   b. Vision is a function of the eye and brain working together, and the process is universal for everyone with the ability to see.
   c. Vision is done solely through the eyes, and nearly everyone has biological eyes.
   d. Vision works on an emotional level that's universal, and emotions are inherently biological.

3. According to the image above, what is the temperature in Fahrenheit?

_____.

4. After Sheila recently had a coronary artery bypass, her doctor encouraged her to switch to a plant-based diet to avoid foods loaded with cholesterol and saturated fats. Sheila's doctor has given her a list of foods she can purchase in order to begin making healthy dinners, which excludes dairy (cheese, yogurt, cream) eggs, and meat. The doctor's list includes the following: pasta, marinara sauce, tofu, rice, black beans, tortilla chips, guacamole, corn, salsa, rice noodles, stir-fry vegetables, teriyaki sauce, quinoa, potatoes, yams, bananas, eggplant, pizza crust, cashew cheese, almond milk, bell pepper, and tempeh.

Which of the following dishes can Sheila make that will be okay for her to eat?

    a. Eggplant parmesan with a salad
    b. Veggie pasta with marinara sauce
    c. Egg omelet with no cheese and bell peppers
    d. Quinoa burger with cheese and French fries.

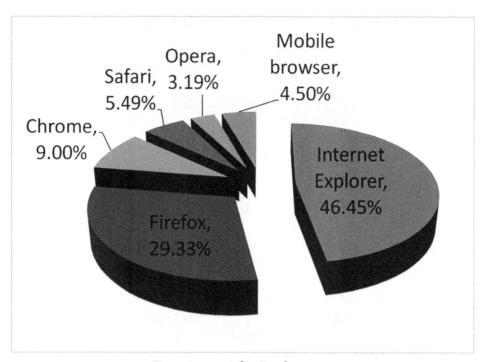

Browser usage for October 2011

5. According to the pie chart above, which browser is most used on Wikimedia in October 2011?

_____

*Answer Question 6 based on the following advertisement.*

*For Question 6, answer True, False, or Not Given.*

6. Does the following statement agree with the information contained in the advertisement?

A customer can buy a single screwdriver for $1.

———

*Answer Question 7 based on the following movie review.*

*The Workplace* is a smash hit, breaking the recent trend of big budget superhero movies dominating at the box office. The movie's protagonist, Steve, is a politically incorrect yet lovable manager of a small town bookstore. Rather than focusing on a dramatic conflict, this movie captures the beauty of everyday life as Steve tries to keep a failing business alive. *The Workplace* is a movie your whole family will enjoy, and I wholeheartedly give it my stamp of approval.

*For Question 7, answer Yes, No, or Not Given.*

7. Does the following statement accurately reflect the movie reviewer's views on *The Workplace?*

The reviewer enjoyed *The Workplace* more than recent big budget superhero movies.

———

*Answer Questions 8 and 9 based on the following notice from an apartment building's property manager.*

A. Several tenants have recently complained about people smoking in front of the building. The smoke has apparently been so heavy that it drifts through the front doors and into the lobby. As you all know, our building has a strict no smoking policy.

B. When I received these complaints, I informed all the smokers in the building about these complaints. They all said they didn't smoke directly in front of the building, but several said they have seen teenagers smoking underneath our building's awning in recent days.

C. However, the complaining tenants still want to formally ban smoking within 25 feet of the building. This measure will be voted upon at our next tenant shareholder meeting. One of the smokers claimed this measure would violate a city ordinance that allows smoking on public sidewalks, and he promised to challenge the measure if it were passed.

D. Therefore I encourage you to attend our next tenant shareholder meeting to discuss this measure as well as our usual business. The meeting will take place next Monday at 7 PM in the lobby.

E. Sincerely,

F. Joe, Property Manager

*For Questions 8 and 9, answer the questions by using the letters next to the paragraph.*

8. Which paragraph mentions a city ordinance that allows smoking on public sidewalks?

9. Which paragraph includes details about the complaints made to the property manager?

*Answer Questions 10 and 11 based on the following emergency bulletin.*

**A. Incident Report**

On the night of October 31, 2018, an elderly man named Daniel Potter went missing. He was last seen that same night by his wife. Daniel was watching television when his wife said goodnight around 8 PM. Daniel suffers from dementia, and his wife believes he left the house and became confused. Law enforcement believes Daniel is likely still in the area.

B._____

Daniel is 75 years old, and he has a light complexion with blue eyes and brown hair. On the night he was last seen, Daniel was wearing gray sweatpants and a white sweatshirt with a hood. He will likely be walking with a steel cane.

C._____

Please call non-emergency services (311) with any relevant information you might have regarding this incident, but if you see someone matching Daniel's description, please call 911 immediately.

*Use the headlines below to answer questions 10 and 11.*

10. Which heading is the best fit for Paragraph B?

11. Which heading is the best fit for Paragraph C?

I. Emergency Exception

II. Likely Location

III. Contact Information

IV. Eyewitness Observation

V. Physical Condition

VI. Missing Person Description

*Answer Question 12 based on the following advertisement for a music festival.*

The greatest collection of musical talent the world has ever seen is coming to our town next Friday night, and we have two extra tickets! Deshaun Jackson (A), a pop sensation, will be the opening act, and that's only the beginning! Alexandra Maine (B) will then hit the stage to show everyone what country music is all about. The festival will conclude with a collaboration between the heavy metal band Iron Guardian (C) and the famed opera singer Enrico Fleming (D). We will sell the pair of tickets for $200 to whoever responds first, so act NOW!

*For Question 12, answer the questions by using the letters next to the musical acts.*

12. Which musical act is the best match for the characteristic described in the following statement? One of these musical acts was recently inducted into the Country Music Hall of Fame.

*Question 13 is based on the following train schedule.*

| Northeast Corridor Train Schedule | | | | |
|---|---|---|---|---|
| Train # | Departs Boston | Arrives New York | Arrives Philadelphia | Arrives Washington DC |
| 1 | 6:00 AM | 9:45 AM | 10:05 AM | 12:10 PM |
| 2 | 10:30 AM | 2:15 PM | N/A | N/A |
| 3 | 3:00 PM | 6:45 PM | 8:05 PM | N/A |
| 4 | 7:30 PM | 11:15 PM | 12:35 AM | 2:40 AM |

*For Question 13, answer using ONLY THREE WORDS.*

13. A salesman in Boston needs to take one of these trains to Philadelphia. What is the latest train the salesman could take from Boston to arrive in Philadelphia before 11 PM?

_____

*Answer Questions 14 based on the following email you received from a friend.*

"Hi! I'm so glad you're going to the art museum. It's my favorite in the city. They have a fabulous collection of Byzantine tapestries that I just know you'll love. When you walk through the entrance hall, take the main corridor to the Egyptian Wing. Then head to your right and go into the Medieval Department. Make sure you don't go left; that's the Modern Art Chamber. Walk through the Medieval Department and you'll find the door to the Byzantine Collection in the northwest corner. Once inside, you can't miss those tapestries. Let me know what you think!"

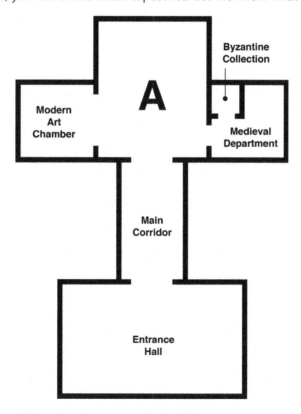

*For Question 14, answer using THREE WORDS OR LESS.*

14. What does "A" represent on the map?

_____

*Answer Question 15 based on the following recipe.*

In a bowl, mix together 1 cup of mayonnaise, 2 cups of sour cream, and 2 ounces of dry vegetable soup mix. Refrigerate the mixture for 10 hours. Add 12 ounces of chopped spinach and 1 cup of chopped water chestnuts to the mixture.

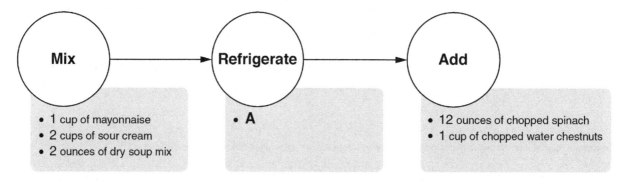

*For Question 15, answer using NO MORE THAN TWO WORDS.*

15. What does "A" represent in the flow chart?

_____

# SERVICE CHANGES

## Track Work Scheduled For **December 1-5**

Travelers should take the **B** or **C** express trains.

Free shuttle buses will be provided at all **B** and **C** stations, and they will take passengers to the **A** stations that are out of service.

*For Question 16, complete the sentence by using NO MORE THAN THREE WORDS.*

16. During the scheduled track work, passengers can travel to local A stops by using a combination of the express trains and _____.

*Questions 17 and 18 are based on the following invitation to a party.*

We are throwing a surprise party for Xavier's birthday on March 9, and we'd love for you to come celebrate with us! As it is a surprise party, make sure you don't say anything to Xavier. If he asks what you're doing, tell him you'll meet him for drinks at Hank's Bar later. We told Xavier everyone is meeting there around 10:00 PM, but he doesn't know that's really the after-party.

The party will be held at Lucy's house. Please arrive well before 5:30 PM. The earlier, the better! Don't worry about being the first guest to arrive. We could always use your help putting up decorations! If you're not sure you'll be able to make it by then, please come after 6:00 PM. Xavier is heading over at 5:45 PM, and we're trying our best to not spoil the surprise.

Please park at Katie's house down the block. Her address is 123 Johnson Avenue, and it's less than a five-minute walk to Lucy's house. Katie has a long driveway, and there's plenty of street parking if it fills up.

RSVP at the website linked at the bottom of this invitation as soon as possible. We're trying to get a guest count before ordering food and drinks.

We look forward to seeing you!

*For Questions 17 and 18, use the answer choices below to best complete the sentences.*

17. Guests who can't arrive before 5:30 PM should ____

18. Aside from arriving early, to avoid spoiling the surprise guests should ____

A. come after 6:00 PM.

B. help decorate before the party.

C. arrive at exactly 5:45 PM.

D. park at Hank's Bar since that's where the after party is being held.

E. only go to the after party at 10:00 PM.

F. park at Katie's house and walk over.

*Answer Question 19 based on the following neighborhood flyer.*

# BLOCK PARTY
## JUNE 17 2018
## 2 PM TO 7 PM

| Family Fun | Delicious Barbeque | Karaoke Competition |
|---|---|---|
| 2-5 PM | 3-6 PM | 5-8 PM |

Thanks to the generous support of local businesses, the Block Party will be free for all families. All are welcome!

*For Question 19, answer True, False, or Not Given.*

19. Does the following statement agree with the information contained in the neighborhood flyer?

Families need to register one month in advance to participate in the Block Party.

_____

*Answer Question 20 based on the following advertisement.*

Tired of spending your hard-earned money on an expensive Internet connection that doesn't even work? We here at Corporate Cable have the solution. Our Internet connection is the fastest in the world, and we would never, ever throttle our valued customers. New subscribers receive their first month for free, and if you're stuck in a contract with your current provider, don't worry, we'll buy out the rest of the contract at no cost to you. Act now to save money! This deal won't last!

*For Question 20, answer Yes, No, or Not Given.*

20. Does the following statement accurately reflect claims made by Corporate Cable in the advertisement?

Corporate Cable is offering a higher quality product at a lower price than its competitors.

_____

## Section 2: Workplace Survival

*Read the following job description for a litigation paralegal, and then answer Questions 21–25.*

### Paralegal Job Description

*Location and Hours*
Paralegals primarily work out of the offices located at 123 Main Street, New York, New York, but they will attend conferences, depositions, and hearings held all over the metropolitan area. Transportation will be provided to off-site locations. Paralegals work Monday to Friday from 9 AM to 6 PM with one hour each day allotted for lunch. When working on pending litigation, paralegals will work up to 10 hours of overtime every week.

**A.**_____

Paralegals are members of litigation teams, and they directly report to the team's supervising attorney. Depending on caseload, paralegals may be asked to work on several teams simultaneously, and they will work on every aspect of a case, including client intake, discovery, trials, and settlements. Paralegals must perform any and all duties assigned by their supervising attorney(s). Typical assignments include researching, conducting interviews, drafting documents, communicating with clients, and tracking deadlines. However, assignments differ from case-to-case.

**B.**_____

Paralegals must hold a bachelor's degree and professional certification from either the National Federation of Paralegal Associations or the National Association of Legal Assistants. Paralegals are individually responsible for ensuring they always hold a valid certification, which might include applying for recertification. In addition, paralegals must be proficient in Microsoft Office suite and Adobe Creative suite.

*Compensation*
Paralegals are paid $50,000 per year, and they are eligible for raises every year. Cost of living raises are automatically applied on an annual basis. Merit raises are negotiable, and they are based on the paralegal's contributions to successful verdicts. Paralegals also receive healthcare, three weeks' paid vacation, and matching 401(k) contributions.

21. Which heading is the best fit for Paragraph A?

22. Which heading is the best fit for Paragraph B?

I. Caseload

II. Certification

III. Education

IV. Requirements

V. Responsibilities

VI. Supervision

*For Question 23, answer using ONLY TWO WORDS.*

23. Where will the firm provide transportation to? _____

*For Question 24, complete the sentence by using ONLY TWO WORDS.*

24. Paralegals work on _____, discovery, trials, and settlements.

*For Question 25, answer True, False, or Not Given.*

25. Does the job description support the following statement?

Paralegals are eligible for two different types of raises.

_____

*Read the following workplace bulletin about how to safely use a nail gun and then answer Questions 26–30.*

There are seven major risk factors that can lead to a nail gun injury. Understanding them will help you to prevent injuries on your jobsites.

**Unintended nail discharge from double fire.**

*Occurs with CONTACT triggers.*

A. The Consumer Product Safety Commission (CPSC) found that contact trigger nailers are susceptible to double firing, especially when trying to accurately place the nailer against the work piece. They found that a second unintended firing can happen faster than the user is able to react and release the trigger. Unintended nails can cause injuries.

B. Double fire can be a particular problem for new workers, who may push hard on the tool to compensate for recoil. It can also occur when the user is working in an awkward position, such as in tight spaces where the gun doesn't have enough space to recoil. The recoil of the gun itself can even cause a non-nail injury in tight spaces if the nail gun hits the user's head or face.

**Unintended nail discharge from knocking the safety contact with the trigger squeezed.**

*Occurs with CONTACT and SINGLE ACTUATION triggers.*

C. Nail guns with contact and single actuation triggers will fire if the trigger is being squeezed and the safety contact tip gets knocked or pushed into an object or person by mistake. For example, a framer might knock his leg going down a ladder or bump into a co-worker passing through a doorway. Contact trigger nailers can release multiple nails, and single actuation trigger nailers can release a single nail to cause injury.

D. Holding or carrying contact trigger or single actuation trigger nail guns with the trigger squeezed increases the risk of unintended nail discharge. Construction workers tend to keep a finger on the trigger because it is more natural to hold and carry an 8-pound nail gun using a full, four-finger grip. Tool manufacturers, however, do warn against it.

**Nail penetration through lumber work piece.**

*Occurs with ALL trigger types.*

E. Nails can pass through a work piece and either hit the worker's hand or fly off as a projectile (airborne) nail. A blow-out nail is one example. Blow-outs can occur when a nail is placed near a knot in the wood. Knots involve a change in wood grain, which creates both weak spots and hard spots that can make the nail change direction and exit the work piece. Nail penetration is especially a concern for placement work where a piece of lumber needs to be held in place by hand. If the nail misses or breaks through the lumber, it can injure the non-dominant hand holding it.

"Nail Gun Safety: A Guide for Construction Contractors," published by Department of Human and Health Services and OSHA,
https://permanent.access.gpo.gov/gpo41185/PDF%20version/NailgunFinal_508_02_optimized.pdf

*For Questions 26 and 27, answer the questions by using the letters next to the paragraph.*

26. Which paragraph mentions an 8-pound nail gun? ____

27. Which paragraph describes how blow-outs occur? ____

*For Questions 28–30, use the answer choices below to best complete the sentences.*

28. Double fire injuries with contact trigger nailers most commonly occur when____

29. Tool manufacturers warn against____

30. Nail penetration injuries can occur when a worker is____

a. a contact trigger nail gun releases a single nail.

b. the worker pushes too hard or is working in an awkward position.

c. holding a piece of lumber in place by hand and the nail misses or breaks through.

d. using an 8-pound nail gun when working with lumber.

e. firing a contact trigger nail gun with a non-dominant hand.

f. the nail gun hits the user in the head or face after recoiling.

g. carrying a single actuation trigger nail gun with a finger on the trigger.

**Section 3: General Reading**

*The next ten questions are based on the following passage:*

For any journey, by rail or by boat, one has a general idea of the direction to be taken, the character of the land or water to be crossed, and of what one will find at the end. So it should be in striking the trail. Learn all you can about the path you are to follow. Whether it is plain or obscure, wet or dry; where it leads; and its length, measured more by time than by actual miles. A smooth, even trail of five miles will not consume the time and strength that must be expended upon a trail of half that length which leads over uneven ground, varied by bogs and obstructed by rocks and fallen trees, or a trail that is all up-hill climbing. If you are a novice and accustomed to walking only over smooth and level ground, you must allow more time for covering the distance than an experienced person would require and must count upon the expenditure of more strength, because your feet are not trained to the wilderness paths with their pitfalls and traps for the unwary, and every nerve and muscle will be strained to secure a safe foothold amid the tangled roots, on the slippery, moss-covered logs, over precipitous rocks that lie in your path. It will take time to pick your way over boggy places where the water oozes up through the thin, loamy soil as through a sponge; and experience alone will teach you which hummock of grass or moss will make a safe stepping-place and will not sink beneath your weight and soak your feet with hidden water. Do not scorn to learn all you can about the trail you are to take . . . It is not that you hesitate to encounter difficulties, but that you may prepare for them. In unknown regions take a responsible guide with you, unless the trail is short, easily followed, and a frequented one. Do not go alone through lonely places; and, being on the trail, keep it and try no explorations of your own, at least not until you are quite familiar with the country and the ways of the wild.

## Blazing the Trail

A woodsman usually blazes his trail by chipping with his axe the trees he passes, leaving white scars on their trunks, and to follow such a trail you stand at your first tree until you see the blaze on the next, then go that and look for the one farther on; going in this way from tree to tree you keep the trail though it may, underfoot, be overgrown and indistinguishable.

If you must make a trail of your own, blaze it as you go by bending down and breaking branches of trees, underbrush, and bushes. Let the broken branches be on the side of bush or tree in the direction you are going, but bent down away from that side, or toward the bush, so that the lighter underside of the leaves will show and make a plain trail. Make these signs conspicuous and close together, for in returning, a dozen feet without the broken branch will sometimes confuse you, especially as everything has a different look when seen from the opposite side. By this same token it is a wise precaution to look back frequently as you go and impress the homeward-bound landmarks on your memory. If in your wanderings you have branched off and made ineffectual or blind trails which lead nowhere, and, in returning to camp, you are led astray by one of them, do not leave the false trail and strike out to make a new one, but turn back and follow the false trail to its beginning, for it must lead to the true trail again. Don't lose sight of your broken branches.

Excerpt from *On the Trail* by Lina Beard and Adelia Belle Beard

31. What part of the text is the girl most likely emulating in the image?
   a. Building a trap
   b. Setting up camp
   c. Blazing the trail
   d. Picking berries to eat

32. According to the passage, what does the author say about unknown regions?
   a. You should try and explore unknown regions in order to learn the land better.
   b. Unless the trail is short or frequented, you should take a responsible guide with you.
   c. All unknown regions will contain pitfalls, traps, and boggy places.
   d. It's better to travel unknown regions by rail rather than by foot.

33. Which statement is NOT a detail from the passage?
   a. Learning about the trail beforehand is imperative.
   b. Time will differ depending on the land.
   c. Once you are familiar with the outdoors you can go places on your own.
   d. Be careful of wild animals on the trail you are on.

34. In the last paragraph, which of the following does the author suggest when being led astray by a false trail?
   a. Bend down and break the branches off trees, underbrush, and bushes.
   b. Ignore the false trail and strike out to make a new one.
   c. Follow the false trail back to its beginning so that you can rediscover the real trail.
   d. Make the signs conspicuous so that you won't be confused when you turn around.

*For Questions 35 and 36, complete the sentence based on the passage using ONLY ONE WORD.*

35. When preparing for a trail, it's important to know: where the trail _____, how long it takes to travel, whether it is plain or obscure, and whether it is wet or dry.

36. A trail that is all-uphill climbing will consume more time and energy than a _____, even trail that is twice as long.

*For Question 37, answer Yes, No, or Not Given.*

37. Does the following statement agree with the claims of the writer?

Novices expend more strength traveling on wilderness paths because their feet become strained trying to secure a safe foothold.

_____

*For Question 38, refer to the following reader's notes, which are based on the passage. Complete the reader's notes by using ONE WORD ONLY.*

38. In boggy places

   - water oozes up through thin, loamy soil

   - like walking across a sponge

   - need to find a safe _____ so don't sink beneath weight

*For Question 39, answer using ONLY ONE WORD.*

39. Who usually blazes a trail by chipping trees with an axe, leaving white scars on the trunks of trees? _____

*For Question 40, answer True, False, or Not Given.*

40. Does the following statement agree with the information contained in the passage?

When blazing your own trail, it's a good idea to look back frequently and try to remember landmarks. _____

# Writing

**First Task**

Test takers are encouraged to spend 20 minutes on this task.

> About twice a week on your way to work you see a crash or near-crash at the same intersection of 24th street and 8th boulevard. You have also had close calls at this intersection. The issue is that the cars that sit on 8th boulevard do not have a stoplight, so they become desperate sitting at the busy intersection at 24th street and decide to risk turning out in the middle of the lane even when there are cars approaching. You have to go through this intersection every day on your way to work, and you're sure there is an appropriate solution to this problem.

Prepare a letter of at least 150 words to a city official. Cover the following items in your letter:

- Briefly paraphrase the situation
- Express your opinion on the situation
- Offer a solution to the situation
- Address information should not be included.

Begin the letter in the following way:

To Whom it May Concern:

**Second Task**

Write an essay of at least 250 words on the topic below:

> Substance abuse recovery centers in Florida have doubled in the past two years. Additionally, the centers that already existed are filled to the maximum occupancy. In order to accommodate the patients, some recovery centers are expanding their residencies and adding more staff. The reason for this rise in recovery centers speaks to the state of our nation with the abuse of drugs and alcohol. The substance abuse problem is worse than ever before and will only continue to grow if we allow the trafficking and consumption of drugs to go unpunished.

Write a response in which you identify your stance on the argument above. Once you've identified your stance, use concrete evidence to support your argument.

# *Speaking*

**Part 1**

What are some of your favorite foods to eat and to cook?

**Part 2**

| *Candidate Task Card* |
|---|
| Describe a family activity or cultural tradition that's important to you. |
| Discuss when it started, how long you've participated in it, and why you value it. |

**Part 3**

How have your family interactions and traditions changed as a result of travel?

# General Training Answers

## *Listening*

**1. B:** The employer called the meeting to ask the employee about Peter and explain why he was terminated. All the remaining topics—previous work experience, current workload, and dinner plans—were mentioned in the conversation, but they were not the main focus.

**2. D:** Peter was fired for threatening to falsify his coworkers' reports and then carrying out that threat. He was asking his coworkers out on dates and then retaliating when they said no. Peter did invite the employee to dinner and spend a lot of time at her desk, but those weren't the direct reasons for his termination. Peter did threaten his coworkers, but not with violence.

**3. D:** The employee describes Peter as being "very helpful" in her transition into a new role. That's why she is so surprised when the employer mentions the complaints. Whether Peter is the employee's direct supervisor is never mentioned, and the employee didn't experience similar harassment at her previous job, though she does say her previous bosses might not have noticed the discrepancy. There is also no romantic relationship—the employee is married to someone else, and she declined Peter's dinner invitation.

**4. B:** The employee forgets to tell her employer that Peter invited her on a date. When initially asked about Peter, she only mentions how helpful Peter was during her transition. Peter's helpfulness is the reason she's surprised when the employer mentions the complaints. Before her employer told her, she didn't know Peter tampered with her reports, and she doesn't hide the reason why Peter was at her desk.

**5. Fire:** The conversation is about how Peter harassed employees and falsified reports. The employer asks the employee about whether Peter had harassed her, but the investigation had already been completed and Peter had already been terminated. At the end of the conversation, the employer describes how she had to *fire* Peter earlier that day. Thus, *fire* is the correct answer.

**6. Complaints:** Peter was asking employees out on dates, and when they refused to go out with him, he threatened to falsify their reports. In addition, Peter made good on his threats and actually lowered his colleagues' customer reviews, including those of the employee in the conversation. In response to this harassment, several employees filed *complaints* against Peter. Thus, *complaints* is the correct answer.

**7. Reports:** While the employee's colleagues filed complaints after being threatened, Peter never overtly threatened the employee. As such, the employer didn't know if Peter had threatened the employee until they noticed Peter had changed customer reviews to falsify *reports*. Thus, *reports* is the correct answer.

**8. Dinner:** The employer is seeking to determine if Peter personally harassed the employee. After the employer mentions Peter's pattern of harassment, the employee mentions how Peter had asked her to go out to *dinner*, but the employee declined his invitation since she was married. Thus, *dinner* is the correct answer.

**9. Email:** The employer begins the conversation by thanking the employee for making time to meet them, meaning that the employer had reached out to the employee. In response, the employee mentions how the employer's *email* had been mysterious. Thus, *email* is the correct answer.

**10. Desk:** The employee describes how Peter had been very helpful in easing her transition at the company, particularly in terms of how the office worked. Prior to the description of this relationship, the employer mentions how Peter had spent a lot of time around the employee's *desk*. Thus, *desk* is the correct answer.

**11. A:** The judge was deciding whether the schools could continue applying the doctrine of "separate but equal," a doctrine that the lawsuit was specifically brought to challenge. The question wasn't whether schools should be concerned with their students' mental development; instead, it was whether segregation harms mental development. Likewise, the judge wasn't questioning whether some races are inferior; the judge was questioning what equality means. The court has the power to change school policies; the decision is about whether they will.

**12. B:** The judge concludes that the doctrine of "separate but equal" has "no place" in schools because it harms children's education and psychological development. Segregation was not already illegal; that's why the case was being appealed. Choices *C* and *D* are the opposite of what the judge concludes.

**13. A:** In segregated school systems in the United States in the twentieth century, schoolchildren were separated based on race. Black students like the ones who were at the center of this lawsuit were forced to attend segregated schools with inferior infrastructure and resources.

**14. C:** As the judge states, segregation naturally led to a "sense of inferiority," which "affects the motivation of a child to learn." Choices *A* and *B* were often true, but they weren't described by the judge. Choice *D* is not true.

**15. Schools:** The court decision is about racial segregation. According to the judge, Black schoolchildren were petitioning the court to gain admission into public *schools*, which were segregated based on race. Thus, *schools* is the correct answer.

**16. Black:** The judge describes how legal representatives of Black schoolchildren brought the legal action to end racial segregation in public schools. Prior to this decision, only white schoolchildren were permitted to attend certain schools. As such, it was Black schoolchildren who were prohibited from attending the public schools in question. Thus, *Black* is the correct answer.

**17. Segregation:** The judge mentions the case of *Plessy v. Ferguson* at the end of his decision. Groundbreaking psychological studies led the judge to overturn *Plessy*. Since the judge decided against the racial segregation of public schools, it can be inferred that the *Plessy* case created the legal basis for racial segregation. Thus, *segregation* is the correct answer.

**18. Inferiority:** According to the judge, psychological studies demonstrated that racial segregation disproportionately harmed Black schoolchildren. The judge describes how racial segregation undermines the educational and mental development of Black schoolchildren. More specifically, the judge held that racial segregation creates a sense of inferiority amongst Black schoolchildren. Thus, *inferiority* is the correct answer.

**19. Integrated:** After describing how racial segregation frustrates educational and mental development, the judge adds that segregation deprives Black schoolchildren of the benefit of attending a racially integrated school system. Unlike segregated school systems, racially integrated school systems are beneficial for all children. Thus, *integrated* is the correct answer.

**20. Equal:** At the end of the decision, the judge provides legal reasoning for overturning *Plessy v. Ferguson*. Given the psychological harm segregation inflicts on black schoolchildren, the judge overturns Plessy and prohibits racial segregation, including its doctrine of "separate but equal." Thus, *equal* is the correct answer.

**21. A:** The main topic of conversation is academic writing, specifically how the student can do better on the next assignment. Francisco Franco and paper topics are discussed, but they aren't the main topic. The professor doesn't describe the grading philosophy.

**22. B:** At the beginning of the conversation, the professor says, "A strong thesis statement is critical for academic writing." The professor would likely agree with the other choices, but she doesn't characterize any of them as "critical for academic writing."

**23. D:** After looking at the student's paper, the professor says, "Your thesis should tell the reader what the paper is about." The professor doesn't say a thesis needs to be written in a neutral tone, and it's unclear whether the thesis functions as part of the introduction or the whole introduction. According to the professor, an appropriate thesis is one or two sentences, not paragraphs.

**24. D:** According to the professor, the student's thesis was a run-on sentence, didn't fit with the rest of the paper, and included two pieces of evidence that weren't mentioned again. The professor does not identify spelling errors as a problem with the last paper's thesis statement.

**25. Thesis:** The professor is most critical of the student's thesis. According to the professor, the student's thesis was a run-on sentence and included evidence that went unmentioned in the rest of the paper. In sum, the professor asserts that the student wrote an unclear thesis. Additionally, the professor's suggested improvement is to write a clear and concise thesis statement. Thus, *thesis* is the correct answer.

**26. Sentence:** The professor describes the student's thesis statement as a run-on sentence. To improve the thesis statement, the professor advises the student to write one or two sentences that clearly states the paper's central message. Thus, *sentence* is the correct answer.

**27. Central:** After explaining why a thesis statement is critical for strong academic writing, the professor describes the importance of tailoring the thesis statement to the paper's central message. The student's thesis statement references evidence that isn't mentioned again in the paper, so the thesis doesn't support the paper's central message. Thus, *central* is the correct answer.

**28. Fascism:** When the professor asks the student if they chose a topic for their next paper, the student explains their selection of *fascism* from the list of political ideologies. According to the student, the paper will focus on how fascist politicians exploit the public's economic anxieties. Thus, *fascism* is the correct answer.

**29. Overall organization:** At the tail end of the conversation, the professor encourages the student to come back with any questions and mentions two ways for the student to better reach their potential. First, the student needs to write a strong thesis statement. Second, the student needs to improve their paper's overall organization. Thus, *overall organization* is the correct answer.

**30. Adolf Hitler:** The student says that they are leaning toward writing about Francisco Franco. However, says the student, if there aren't enough quality sources to write about Franco, their back-up plan is to focus on Adolf Hitler. Thus, *Adolf Hitler* is the correct answer.

**31. B:** The lecture's primary purpose is to explain the power of visual propaganda, especially in relation to text-based propaganda. Much of the lecture is devoted to explaining how online visual propaganda attracts more attention, increases recall, and expands its audience. The professor is concerned with terrorism and extremism, but the primary focus is how those groups use propaganda. Prohibiting propaganda is not mentioned in the lecture, and although the professor would likely support more research on propaganda, calling for more studies isn't the primary purpose.

**32. D:** The early studies considered propaganda to be a top-down transaction, while the more recent studies believe it's a two-way transaction. The professor states that the two-way transaction is between the propaganda's creator and its target, and that the target plays an "active role in the production of meaning." It can be inferred that the top-down model viewed the propaganda's creator as the source of meaning. The other choices could all possibly be true, but they aren't as strongly supported as Choice *D*.

**33. B:** The professor believes that vision is a biological process that is a function of the eye and brain working together. The process is universal, because it works for everyone with the ability to see. The other choices are either wholly inaccurate or only partially true.

**34. A:** The professor argues that visual propaganda attracts more attention, increases recall, and expands its audience, as compared to text-based propaganda. Based on its numerous advantages, we can infer that visual propaganda is probably more cost effective, but the professor doesn't directly address reducing costs.

**35. G:** At the beginning of the lecture, the professor differentiates between propaganda and persuasion. According to the professor, propaganda is a type of persuasion, but propaganda can be clearly identified based on its intentional and directed dissemination of particular ideas. This is far more specific than the definition for persuasion, so Choice *F* is incorrect. *Propaganda* best completes the first sentence of the summary because the rest of the sentence provides the definition of propaganda. Thus, Choice *G* is the correct answer.

**36. D:** In the middle of the lecture, the professor asserts that visual images trigger powerful, immediate, and emotionally visceral responses in viewers. As such, the type of reaction mentioned in the summary has to be emotional. Thus, Choice *D* is the correct answer.

**37. B:** The professor attributes the emotionally visceral impact of visual propaganda to the combined role of the brain and the eye when people view images. While propaganda has a cultural component, the professor doesn't connect culture to propaganda's visceral impact, so Choice *C* is incorrect. Instead, the professor explicitly states that vision is a biological function, and that that is why it triggers such an emotionally visceral response. Thus, Choice *B* is the correct answer.

**38. A:** Near the end of the lecture, the professor describes visual images' ability to attract attention and expand the audience for propaganda. Although visual-based propaganda can increase the engagement of viewers, the professor doesn't explicitly make this point. Therefore, Choice *E* is incorrect. The professor is much more focused on how visual images expand the audience of propaganda, particularly when the propaganda is directed toward a young and illiterate audience. Thus, Choice *A* is the correct answer.

**39. Brain:** In the middle of the lecture, the professor explains that vision is a biological function that inherently distorts how people see and interact with the world. Specifically, the combined role of the brain and the eyes in the interpretation of visual images creates powerful, immediate, and emotionally visceral response. Thus, *brain* is the correct answer.

**40. Text:** At the end of the lecture, the professor describes how visual images lead to superior message recall because the act of viewing an image bypasses logical reasoning. In direct contrast, text-based propaganda involves series of claims and evidence that people are trained to resist. Thus, *text* is the correct answer.

# *Reading*

**1. C:** Personification. The chapter on Literature and Language Use has a subsection, "Figurative Speech." The sections located under Figurative Speech all have to do with language that uses words or phrases that are different from their literal interpretation. Personification is included in figurative speech, which means giving inanimate objects human characteristics. Nouns, agreement, and syntax all have to do with grammar and usage, and are not considered figurative language.

**2. B:** To convince the audience that judges holding their positions based on good behavior is a practical way to avoid corruption.

**3.** 62° Fahrenheit.

**4. B:** Veggie pasta with marinara sauce. Choices *A* and *D* are incorrect because they both contain cheese, and the doctor gave Sheila a list *without* dairy products. Choice *C* is incorrect because the doctor is also having Sheila stay away from eggs, and the omelet has eggs in it. Choice *B* is the best answer because it contains no meat, dairy, or eggs.

**5. D:** According to the pie chart, Internet Explorer (I.E.) is the most used browser in October 2011. Following that is Firefox with 23.6% usage, Chrome with 20.6% usage, and Safari with 11.2% usage.

**6. False:** The advertisement is offering screwdrivers for $1. However, customers must buy two screwdrivers to receive that sale price. That condition is noted with an asterisk, and the relevant information is provided at the bottom of the advertisement. Thus the customer cannot buy a single screwdriver for $1, so the correct answer is False.

**7. Not Given:** The reviewer doesn't give an opinion on whether he enjoyed *The Workplace* more than big budget superhero movies. He only notes that *The Workplace* broke a recent trend of big budget superhero movies. Thus, the correct answer is Not Given.

**8. C:** Paragraph C is the only paragraph to mention a city ordinance. The relevant sentences say: "One of the smokers claimed this measure would violate a city ordinance that allows smoking on public sidewalk, and he promised to challenge the measure if it were passed." Thus, Paragraph C is the correct answer.

**9. A:** While other paragraphs reference the complaint, Paragraph A is the only paragraph where there are details about the complaints made to the property manager. The relevant sentences say: "Several tenants have recently complained about people smoking in front of the building. The smoke has apparently been so heavy that it drifts through the front doors and into the lobby." Thus, Paragraph A is the correct answer.

**10. VI:** Based on the two existing headings, the heading should be one that summarizes the paragraph directly underneath it. Paragraph B describes the physical appearance and clothing of Daniel, the missing person. Thus, the best heading is Missing Person Description, so Choice *VI* is the correct answer. Although the paragraph mentions his physical condition, that is only part of the paragraph's content.

**11. III:** Based on the two existing headings, the heading will be one that summarizes the paragraph directly underneath it. Paragraph C describes who people should contact if they see or know anything about Daniel. Thus the best heading is Contact Information, so Choice *III* is the correct answer. The paragraph does mention a non-emergency line, but Emergency Exception (Choice *II*) doesn't accurately describe the paragraph's substance or purpose.

**12. B:** The advertisement mentions the genres of all four musical acts. Deshaun Jackson (Choice *A*) plays pop music; Alexandra Maine (Choice *B*) plays country music; Iron Guardian (Choice *C*) plays heavy metal; and Enrico Fleming (Choice *D*) is an opera singer. Because Alexandra Maine is the only musical act that plays country music, she is most likely to have been recently inducted into the Country Music Hall of Fame. Thus, Choice *B* is the correct answer.

**13. Train Number 3:** The salesman needs to arrive in Philadelphia before 11 PM, and he wants to take a train that leaves Boston at the latest possible time. Train Number 1 arrives in Philadelphia at 10:05 AM, which is before 11 PM. Train Number 2 doesn't arrive in Philadelphia at all. Train Number 3 arrives in Philadelphia at 8:05 PM, which is also before 11 PM. Train Number 4 arrives in Boston at 12:35 AM, which is after 11 PM. So the only trains that would work are Train Number 1 and Train Number 3, and Train Number 3 leaves Boston at a later time in the day. Thus, Train Number 3 is the correct answer.

**14. Egyptian Wing:** The main corridor leads into the square labeled "A," and the square is located between the Modern Art Chamber and Medieval Department. Thus, based on the directions, "A" must be the Egyptian Wing. You could also arrive at this answer by finding all the other rooms on the map. The Egyptian Wing is the only part of the museum that is not labeled on the map.

**15. 10 hours:** The bullet point marked A is in a circle titled "Refrigerate," and the recipe says to refrigerate the mixture for 10 hours. There is no other reference to refrigeration in the recipe. Thus the correct answer is 10 hours.

**16. Free shuttle buses:** The poster is announcing service changes for the subway. The change is that the A train isn't operating; this fact is represented by a diagonal slash through the A. At the bottom of the poster, there are directions for people who want to reach A stations. The directions say that passengers should take the B or C express trains, and all B and C stations have free shuttle buses to A stations. Thus the completed sentence should read: "During the scheduled track work, passengers can travel to local A stops by using a combination of the express trains and free shuttle buses."

**17. A:** The invitation is very specific about when guests should arrive. According to the second paragraph, guests are supposed to arrive before 5:30 PM, and if they can't make it by then, they should come after 6:00 PM. So, the completed sentence should be: "Guests that can't arrive before 5:30 PM should come after 6:00 PM to avoid spoiling the surprise." Thus, Choice *A* is the correct answer.

**18. F:** The hosts are requesting that guests park at Katie's house, because having too many cars at Lucy's house would spoil the surprise. The invitation also says that guests can easily walk from Katie's house to Lucy's. All that information is in the third paragraph. So the completed sentence should be: "To help avoid drawing attention to the surprise party, guests need to park at Katie's house and walk over." Thus, Choice *F* is the correct answer.

**19. Not Given:** The neighborhood flyer provides a date and time, lists activities, thanks the block party's sponsors, and invites the whole community. However, the flyer never mentions registration of any kind. Thus, the correct answer is Not Given.

**20. Yes:** In the third sentence, the advertisement claims that Corporate Cable provides the fastest Internet in the world. So Corporate Cable is claiming to have a higher quality product than its competition. In the first sentence, the advertisement claims that Corporate Cable's competitors are providing expensive services. The fourth and fifth sentences also claim that customers will save money by switching from competitors to Corporate Cable. Thus, the correct answer is Yes.

**Text 1**

**21. V:** Based on the two existing headings, the heading should summarize the paragraph directly underneath it. Paragraph A describes paralegals' role on litigation teams, relationship to supervisors, and typical assignments. These are a paralegal's responsibilities in the workplace. Thus, Choice V is the correct answer. Although the paragraph does reference paralegals' caseload (Choice I) and supervision (Choice VI), those are only part of their larger responsibilities.

**22. IV:** Based on the two existing headings, we are looking for a heading that summarizes the paragraph directly underneath it. The paragraph under "B" describes the level of education, certification, and technological proficiency paralegal must hold. Repeated use of "must" emphasizes that these are requirements for the position. Thus, Choice IV is the correct answer. While the paragraph mentions certification (Choice II) and education (Choice III), those are only aspects of the requirements to work as a paralegal.

**23. Off-site locations:** The job description only mentions transportation in the first paragraph under the "Location and Hours" heading. That paragraph says: "Transportation will be provided to off-site locations." Remember that hyphenated words only count as one word, so "off-site locations" fits the word count. Thus, "off-site locations" is the correct answer.

**24. Client intake:** The sentence is describing different aspects of a legal case, which are described in the paragraph under the "A" heading. The paragraph says: "they will work on every aspect of a case, including client intake, discovery, trials, and settlements." Thus "client intake" is the correct answer.

**25. True:** The job description discusses raises under the "Compensation" heading. The paragraph says: "Cost of living raises are automatically applied on an annual basis. Merit raises are negotiable, and they are based on the paralegal's contributions to successful verdicts." Costs of living raises and merit raises are two different types of raises. Thus, the statement is true.

**Text 2**

**26. D:** Paragraph D is the only paragraph that specifically mentions an 8-pound nail gun. The paragraph says: "Construction workers tend to keep a finger on the trigger because it is more natural to hold and carry an 8-pound nail gun using a full, four-finger grip." Thus, Paragraph D is the correct answer.

**27. E:** Paragraph E describes how blow-outs occur. The paragraph says: "Blow-outs can occur when a nail is placed near a knot in the wood." In addition, blow-outs are not mentioned in any other paragraph. Thus, Paragraph E is the correct answer.

**28. B:** Double fire accidents are described in Paragraphs A and B. The relevant sentence is in Paragraph B, and it says: "Double fire can be a particular problem for new workers who may push hard on the tool to compensate for recoil. It can also occur when the user is working in an awkward position, such as in tight spaces where the gun doesn't have enough space to recoil." So the completed sentence should read: "Double fire injuries with contact trigger nailers most commonly occur when the worker pushes too hard or is working in an awkward position." Thus, Choice *B* is the correct answer.

**29. G:** Tool manufacturers are only mentioned in Paragraph D. It says: "Tool manufacturers, however, do warn against it." The "it" is referencing the previous sentence's description of the danger facing workers who hold or carry contact trigger or single actuation trigger nail guns with a finger on the trigger. So the completed sentence should read: Tool manufacturers warn against carrying single actuation trigger nail guns with a finger on the trigger. Thus, Choice *G* is the correct answer.

**30. C:** Nail penetration injuries are described in Paragraph E. The relevant sentences say: "Nail penetration is especially a concern for placement work where a piece of lumber needs to be held in place by hand. If the nail misses or breaks through the lumber it can injure the non-dominant hand holding it." So, the completed sentence should read: Nail penetration injuries can occur when a worker is holding a piece of lumber in place by hand and the nail misses or breaks through. Thus, Choice *C* is the correct answer.

**31. C:** The section that is talked about in the text is blazing the trail, which is Choice *C.* The passage states that one must blaze the trail by "bending down and breaking branches of trees, underbrush, and bushes." The girl in the image is bending a branch in order to break it so that she can use it to "blaze the trail" so she won't get lost.

**32. B:** Choice *B* is the best answer here; the sentence states "In unknown regions take a responsible guide with you, unless the trail is short, easily followed, and a frequented one." Choice *A* is incorrect; the passage does not state that you should try and explore unknown regions. Choice *C* is incorrect; the passage talks about trails that contain pitfalls, traps, and boggy places, but it does not say that *all* unknown regions contain these things. Choice *D* is incorrect; the passage mentions "rail" and "boat" as means of transport at the beginning, but it does not suggest it is better to travel unknown regions by rail.

**33. D:** Choice *D* is correct; it may be real advice an experienced hiker would give to an inexperienced hiker. However, the question asks about details in the passage, and this is not in the passage. Choice *A* is incorrect; we do see the author encouraging the reader to learn about the trail beforehand . . . "wet or dry; where it leads; and its length." Choice *B* is also incorrect, because we do see the author telling us the time will lengthen with boggy or rugged places opposed to smooth places. Choice *C* is incorrect; at the end of the passage, the author tells us "do not go alone through lonely places . . . unless you are quite familiar with the country and the ways of the wild."

**34. C:** The best answer here is Choice *C:* "Follow the false trail back to its beginning so that you can rediscover the real trail." Choices *A* and *D* are represented in the text; but this is advice on how to blaze a trail, not what to do when being led astray by a false trail. Choice *B* is incorrect; this is the opposite of what the text suggests doing.

**35. Leads:** The question asks for one word to complete the sentence. The sentence describes what people should know when preparing for a trail. Early in the passage's first paragraph, it says: "Learn all you can about the path you are to follow. Whether it is plain or obscure, wet or dry; where it leads; and its length, measured more by time than by actual miles." The sentence in this question mentions everything except "where it leads," and the word "it" clearly refers to the trail. Thus, the completed sentence should read: "When preparing for a trail, it's important to know: where the trail LEADS, how long it takes to travel, whether it is plain or obscure, and whether it is wet or dry."

**36. Smooth:** The question asks for one word to complete the sentence. Early in the passage's first paragraph, it says: "A smooth, even trail of five miles will not consume the time and strength that must be expended upon a trail of half that length...that is all up-hill climbing." The question has reversed this sentence from the passage. Thus, the completed sentence should read: "A trail that is all-uphill climbing will consume more time and energy than a SMOOTH, even trail that is twice as long."

**37. Yes:** The question is asking whether the statement agrees with the writer's claim. The first paragraph describes how "every nerve and muscle will be strained to secure a foothold" when you are novice walking on rough ground, so the writer would agree with this claim.

**38. Stepping-place:** The question asks for only one word with which to complete a reader's notes. Boggy places are mentioned in the middle of the first paragraph, and there is a sentence about a "safe stepping-place" that "will not sink beneath your weight." So "stepping-place" best completes the notes. Remember that hyphenated words count as one word.

**39. Woodsman:** The question asks for a one-word answer. The first sentence of the second paragraph describes a woodsman blazing a trail by using his axe.

**40. True:** The question asks whether the statement agrees with the passage. The middle of the passage's final paragraph advises hikers to take a "wise precaution" and "look back frequently as you go."

# General Training Listening Transcripts

## *Passage #1: Employee Conversation*

**(Narrator)** Listen to a conversation between an employee and her employer and then answer the questions.

**(Employer)** Thank you for making time to meet with me. I know it's been a long day. And it's hard not to get bogged down with work this time of year.

**(Employee)** No problem. What is it you wanted to talk about? Your email was a little mysterious.

**(Employer)** I'm sorry about that. We were in the middle of a delicate situation, so I was trying to spare most of the details. I didn't want to worry you.

**(Employee)** Worry me about what?

**(Employer)** It's something to do with Peter. I've noticed he's spending a lot of time at your desk. Is there anything troublesome that I should know about?

**(Employee)** Not that I'm aware of. He's always seemed like a nice guy. In fact, he was a big help when I first got this job. It was hard transitioning at first, since the pace here is much faster than my previous job. He helped me figure out where things are and how things work around the office.

**(Employer)** Okay. I was hoping nothing weird was going on. We've unfortunately had some complaints recently.

**(Employee)** Complaints?

**(Employer)** Yes, several employees have filed formal complaints. Apparently, Peter has been asking them out on dates, and if they say no, he's threatened to falsify their customer reviews. Unfortunately, those threats were not empty. He altered the records of several employees over the last few months. That's how it came to my attention.

**(Employee)** Oh, wow. I had no idea. Now that you mention it, Peter did ask me to have dinner with him last week. He didn't threaten me, but he did seem upset when I said I was married and didn't feel comfortable going out with him.

**(Employer)** I'm glad he didn't threaten you, but unfortunately, he did tamper with your reports. I noticed you were receiving low scores, so I contacted our customers. Everyone I spoke to said you were doing a terrific job, and they had no complaints.

**(Employee)** I can't believe he'd do such a thing. He seemed like such a great guy.

**(Employer)** Yeah, I thought the same. We didn't receive any complaints against him until this happened. So it will be hard to lose him at the moment, considering our current workload, but I couldn't let this continue. So, I fired Peter earlier today. I just wanted to let you know what happened.

**(Employee)** Thanks for looking into the matter and letting me know. I don't think my previous bosses would have noticed the discrepancy in the reports.

**(Employer)** Oh anytime. I'm just sorry this happened.

## Passage #2: Court Decision

**(Narrator)** Listen to the judge delivering his court's decision and then answer the questions.

**(Judge)** In each of the cases, [black school children], through their legal representatives, seek the aid of the courts in obtaining admission to the public schools of their community on a non-segregated basis. In each instance, they had been denied admission to schools attended by white children under laws requiring or permitting segregation according to race.

To separate them from others of similar age and qualifications solely because of their race generates a feeling of inferiority as to their status in the community that may affect their hearts and minds in a way unlikely ever to be undone. Segregation of white and [black] children in public schools has a detrimental effect upon the [black] children. The impact is greater when it has the sanction of the law, for the policy of separating the races is usually interpreted as denoting the inferiority of the [black] group. A sense of inferiority affects the motivation of a child to learn. Segregation with the sanction of law, therefore, has a tendency to retard the educational and mental development of [black] children and to deprive them of some of the benefits they would receive in a racially integrated school system. Whatever may have been the extent of psychological knowledge at the time of *Plessy v. Ferguson,* this finding is amply supported by modern authority. Any language in *Plessy v. Ferguson* contrary to this finding is rejected.

We conclude that, in the field of public education, the doctrine of "separate but equal" has no place.

## Passage #3: Professor/Student Conversation

**(Narrator)** Listen to the conversation between the student and professor and then answer the questions.

**(Student)** Good morning, Professor. Do you have a second? I have a couple of questions about the previous assignment.

**(Professor)** Sure thing.

**(Student)** Well, on my last paper you took off points for a weak thesis statement, and I was hoping that you could show me how to write a better one so I don't make the same mistake again.

**(Professor)** Of course. Did you bring a copy of that assignment?

**(Student)** Yes, here it is.

**(Professor)** Ah, yes. I remember marking this paper. The thesis itself isn't too bad, but the rest of the paper doesn't really follow it. Your thesis should tell the reader what the paper is about in one or two sentences, and the rest of the paper should support this central message.

**(Student)** What do you mean my paper doesn't follow the thesis?

**(Professor)** The thesis you wrote in your paper relies on two specific pieces of evidence. But those pieces of evidence are never mentioned again in the rest of the paper. It's also a run-on sentence. A thesis should be clear and concise.

**(Student)** Oh, okay. That makes a lot of sense. Thanks.

**(Professor)** Anytime. Have you picked a topic for your next paper?

**(Student)** Yes, I chose fascism from the list of political ideologies you provided us, and I'm focusing on how fascist politicians exploit the public's economic anxiety.

**(Professor)** That sounds very interesting! But it also seems a tad too broad. Have you thought about selecting a specific country or time period to focus on?

**(Student)** Definitely. I'm leaning toward the Francisco Franco era, but if I don't find enough quality sources, I'll do Adolf Hitler.

**(Professor)** Sounds good. If you have any questions while writing, please don't hesitate to ask. I think you have a lot of potential if you improve your thesis and overall organization.

**(Student)** Will do. Thanks again.

## *Passage #4: Lecture*

**(Narrator)** Listen to the professor's lecture and then answer the questions.

**(Professor)** Propaganda is a form of directed persuasion that places the intent of the speaker or propagandist at the center of inquiry. The distinctive features separating propaganda from persuasion involve intent, form, and function. Related scholarship describes persuasion as an interactive process that seeks mutual recognition, engagement, and consensus between speaker and audience, while describing propaganda as directed or intentional attempts to "disseminate or promote particular ideas." Early studies proposed propaganda as a top-down transaction, but more recent inquiries present propaganda as a two-way transaction in which elite propagandizing interacts with target audiences who play an active role in the production of meaning.

The basis for the visual image, vision itself, is biological and is therefore universal across cultures. The vast majority of human beings process that which they see and the way they experience the world visually, which in turn, is a function of the way the eye and the brain work together. . . . Humans process images more quickly than text, making images more emotionally visceral and responses to images frequently more immediate and powerful than responses to text.

Visual images not only attract the attention of viewers, but they also expand the audience base for the messages of media campaigns. Images can attract the attention of younger or illiterate audience members who lack sufficient reading skills for efficient processing of written text. As many terrorist and other extremist groups target audiences from regions with large youth populations and high illiteracy rates in their online propaganda campaigns, understanding visual message strategies becomes an imperative for realizing the full extent of what such groups are communicating.

Beyond increasing both the attention and the potential size of target audiences, the use of visual images in persuasive campaigns also heightens message recall. Experimental studies demonstrate that viewers recall visual information at higher rates than information that either auditory or textual channels deliver. Scholars explain why by noting that viewers appear to bypass logic and accept images at face value. Text, by contrast, "consists of claims, warrants, and evidence, which people are trained to resist."

# Academic Test

## *Listening*

Directions: The Listening section measures your ability to understand conversations and lectures in English. In this test, you will listen to several pieces of content and answer questions after each one. The questions typically ask about the main idea and supporting details. Some questions ask about a speaker's purpose or attitude. Answer the questions based on what is stated or implied by the speakers.

Listen to all of these passages here:

**www.apexprep.com/ielts**

Note that on the actual test, you can take notes while you listen and use your notes to help you answer the questions. Your notes will not be scored.

For your convenience, the transcripts of all of the audio passages are provided after the answer explanations. However, on the actual test, no such transcripts will be provided.

**Passage 1: Tourist Conversation**

**Listen Here: www.apexprep.com/ielts**

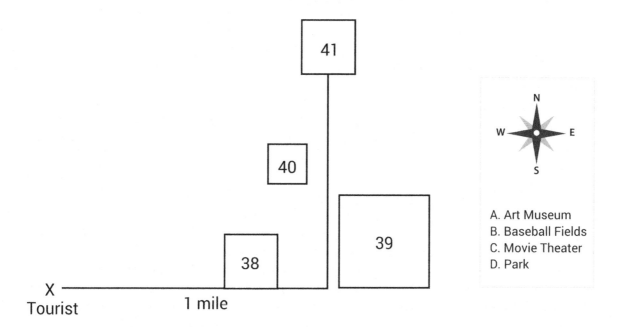

*Questions 1–4: Choose the letter from the map legend that matches the diagram.*

       1. (Box 38)_____

       2. (Box 39)_____

       3. (Box 40)_____

       4. (Box 41)_____

5. What does the tourist mean when they say, "I keep getting turned around"?
    a. The tourist has never been to this city before.
    b. The tourist is dizzy.
    c. The tourist left their map at the art museum.
    d. The tourist is lost.

6. Why does the tourist repeat the directions back to the local?
    a. The tourist is asking for clarification about whether to take a left or right at the movie theater.
    b. The tourist didn't hear the directions.
    c. The tourist wants to confirm that they understand the directions.
    d. The tourist doesn't understand English very well.

*Questions 7–10: Complete the plan below with NO MORE THAN TWO WORDS per answer.*

| Planned Route |
|---|
| A. Walk east for one ____. |
| B. A giant movie theater will be on your ____. |
| C. Turn left before you get to the ____. |
| D. Again on your left you'll see some ____ before running into the museum. |

**Passage #2: Actor's Monologue**

**Listen Here: www.apexprep.com/ielts**

*Questions 11–15: Complete the notes using the list of words, **A–I**, found below the notes.*

| Notes |
|---|
| • 11. Watson returned to a _____ practice; |
| • 12. former _____ sent Watson regular referrals; and |
| • 13. Watson previously worked closely with _____. |
| • 14. Watson's _____ woke him up, and |
| • 15. he met with the _____. |

A. Bohemian

B. Civil

C. Guard

D. Hatherley

E. Holmes

F. Legal

G. Maid

H. Patients

I. Waburton

*Questions 16–20: Complete the sentences below with NO MORE THAN ONE WORD per answer.*

Watson brought two cases to 16._____: Mr. Hatherley's thumb and Colonel Waburton's madness.

Watson treated a lot of patients who were 17._____ officials.

Watson lived near 18. _____Station.

Watson's work had previously been printed in 19. _____.

Watson and Holmes worked together for years in the 20. _____Street rooms.

**Passage #3: Customer and Employee Conversation**

**Listen Here: www.apexprep.com/ielts**

21. What does the customer come into the store looking for?
    a. A product with vitamin C in it
    b. A product with vitamin A in it
    c. An anti-aging product for the face
    d. A facial product that contains retinol

22. Where is the conversation most likely taking place?
    a. In a city park
    b. In a department store
    c. In someone's living room
    d. At a university career fair

23. Which product does the customer already have at home?
    a. Face wash that contains vitamin C
    b. Moisturizer that contains retinol
    c. Face wash with vitamin C and retinol
    d. Moisturizer with vitamin C and retinol

24. Which product does the employee recommend to the customer?
    a. A product that contains retinol
    b. A product that contains vitamin C
    c. A new facial wash that they're selling
    d. An anti-aging moisturizer

25. According to the employee, what are the benefits of retinol on the skin?
    a. Works to prevent aging from sun damage or from acne
    b. Serves to strip the skin of any dead skin cells for a smoother appearance
    c. Maintains the skin's natural color and moisturizes the skin
    d. Produces new cells, smooths out wrinkles, and minimizes skin damage

*Questions 26–30: Answer the questions below with NO MORE THAN TWO WORDS per answer.*

26. What is the primary benefit of vitamin C for the skin?

27. Which skin issue does the customer specifically mention?

28. What does retinol help the body produce?

29. What does the employee describe as an all-in-one solution to reverse skin damage?

30. What is another name for retinol?

**Passage #4: Politician's Speech**

**Listen Here: www.apexprep.com/ielts**

31. What is the politician's primary purpose?
    a. To outline the Nation's future plans
    b. To ridicule past policies
    c. To cast blame on enemies
    d. To support agriculture

32. What does the politician identify as the government's "greatest primary task"?
    a. Provide adequate currency
    b. Regulate banking
    c. Prohibit foreclosure
    d. Increase employment

33. What can be inferred about the country's economy during this period?
    a. The economy is prosperous.
    b. The economy is relatively healthy.
    c. The economy is experiencing limited turmoil in some sectors.
    d. The economy is in a depression.

34. Which one of the following is NOT an economic problem identified by the politician?
    a. Inefficient land distribution
    b. Speculation with other people's money
    c. A lack of natural resources
    d. A weak currency

35. Which analogy does the politician use to explain the country's economic situation?
    a. The politician compares rescuing the economy with forcing Congress to take aggressive action.
    b. The politician compares rescuing the economy with fighting a war.
    c. The politician compares rescuing the economy with facing fear.
    d. The politician compares rescuing the economy with finding a better use for land.

*Questions 36–38: Complete the flowchart using the list of words, **A-F**, found below the flowchart.*

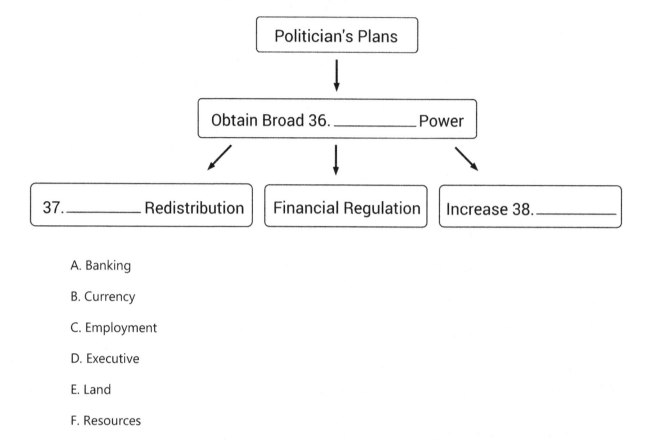

A. Banking

B. Currency

C. Employment

D. Executive

E. Land

F. Resources

*Questions 39–40: Complete the summary below with NO MORE THAN ONE WORD per answer.*

The politician considers facing 39._____ itself is the first step to solution. If 40._____ fails to act, the politician is prepared to treat the economic depression as a war-like emergency, justifying dramatic actions.

# Reading

A variety of question types are used, chosen from the following: multiple choice, identifying information, identifying writer's views/claims, matching information, matching headings, matching features, matching sentence endings, sentence completion, summary completion, note completion, table completion, flow-chart completion, diagram label completion, and short-answer questions.

*Questions 1–13 are based on the following passage:*

The box in which the President sat consisted of two boxes turned into one, the middle partition being removed, as on all occasions when a state party visited the theater. The box was on a level with the dress circle; about twelve feet above the stage. There were two entrances—the door nearest to the wall having been closed and locked; the door nearest the balustrades of the dress circle, and at right angles with it, being open and left open, after the visitors had entered. The interior was carpeted, lined with crimson paper, and furnished with a sofa covered with crimson velvet, three arm chairs similarly covered, and six cane-bottomed chairs. Festoons of flags hung before the front of the box against a background of lace.

President Lincoln took one of the arm-chairs and seated himself in the front of the box, in the angle nearest the audience, where, partially screened from observation, he had the best view of what was transpiring on the stage. Mrs. Lincoln sat next to him, and Miss Harris in the opposite angle nearest the stage. Major Rathbone sat just behind Mrs. Lincoln and Miss Harris. These four were the only persons in the box.

The play proceeded, although "Our American Cousin," without Mr. Sothern, has, since that gentleman's departure from this country, been justly esteemed a very dull affair. The audience at Ford's, including Mrs. Lincoln, seemed to enjoy it very much. The worthy wife of the President leaned forward, her hand upon her husband's knee, watching every scene in the drama with amused attention. Even across the President's face at intervals swept a smile, robbing it of its habitual sadness.

About the beginning of the second act, the mare, standing in the stable in the rear of the theater, was disturbed in the midst of her meal by the entrance of the young man who had quitted her in the afternoon. It is presumed that she was saddled and bridled with exquisite care.

Having completed these preparations, Mr. Booth entered the theater by the stage door; summoned one of the scene shifters, Mr. John Spangler, emerged through the same door with that individual, leaving the door open, and left the mare in his hands to be held until he (Booth) should return. Booth who was even more fashionably and richly dressed than usual, walked thence around to the front of the theater, and went in. Ascending to the dress circle, he stood for a little time gazing around upon the audience and occasionally upon the stage in his usual graceful manner. He was subsequently observed by Mr. Ford, the proprietor of the theater, to be slowly elbowing his way through the crowd that packed the rear of the dress circle toward the right side, at the extremity of which was the box where Mr. and Mrs. Lincoln and their companions were seated. Mr. Ford casually noticed this as a slightly extraordinary symptom of interest on the part of an actor so familiar with the routine of the theater and the play.

Excerpt from *The Life, Crime, and Capture of John Wilkes Booth* by George Alfred Townsend

1. Which of the following best describes the author's attitude toward the events leading up to the assassination of President Lincoln?
    a. Excitement due to the setting and its people
    b. Sadness due to the death of a beloved president
    c. Anger because of the impending violence
    d. Neutrality due to the style of the report

2. What does the author mean by the last sentence in the passage?
    a. Mr. Ford was suspicious of Booth and assumed he was making his way to Mr. Lincoln's box.
    b. Mr. Ford assumed Booth's movement throughout the theater was due to Booth's familiarity with the events of the theater.
    c. Mr. Ford thought that Booth was making his way to the theater lounge to find his companions.
    d. Mr. Ford thought that Booth was elbowing his way to the dressing room to get ready for the play.

3. Given the author's description of the play *Our American Cousin*, which one of the following is most analogous to Mr. Sothern's departure from the theater?

    a. A ballet dancer who leaves the New York City Ballet just before they go on to their final performance

    b. A ballet dancer who is accepted into Julliard but is expelled due to criminal activity.

    c. A lead singer who leaves their band to begin a solo career, and whose former band sees sales drop by 50 percent on their next album

    d. A movie actor who dies in the middle of making a movie, which is then completed by actors who resemble the deceased

4. Based on the organizational structure of the passage, which of the following texts most closely resembles the passage about Booth?

    a. A chronological account in a fiction novel of a woman and a man meeting for the first time

    b. A cause-and-effect text ruminating on the causes of global warming

    c. An autobiography that begins with the subject's death and culminates in his birth

    d. An article about finding a solution to the problem of the Higgs Boson particle

5. Which of the following words, if substituted for the word *festoons* in the first paragraph, would LEAST change the meaning of the sentence?

    a. Feathers

    b. Armies

    c. Adornment

    d. Buckets

6. What is the primary purpose of the passage?

    a. To persuade the audience that John Wilkes Booth killed Abraham Lincoln

    b. To inform the audience of the setting where Lincoln was shot

    c. To narrate the bravery of Lincoln and his last days as president

    d. To recount in detail the events that led up to Abraham Lincoln's death

*Questions 7–8*

    7. Booth walked back out the stable door and came around the theater to enter through the

    _____.

    8. In the first paragraph, the _____ and box are described as being above and to the right side of the stage.

*Questions 9–13: Reading Passage 1 has five sections I–V. Match the correct heading, **A–H**, from the list below to each section.*

| | | |
|---|---|---|
| 9. Section I | A. Crowd-Pleasing Act | F. Presidential Seating Arrangement |
| 10. Section II | B. Third Act | |
| 11. Section III | C. Box Description | G. Theater Stable |
| 12. Section IV | D. Final Curtain | H. Ford's Departure |
| 13. Section V | E. Booth's Entrance | |

The first and most universal change effected in milk is its souring. So universal is this phenomenon that it is generally regarded as an inevitable change which can not be avoided, and, as already pointed out, has in the past been regarded as a normal property of milk. To-day, however, the phenomenon is well understood. It is due to the action of certain of the milk bacteria upon the milk sugar which converts it into lactic acid, and this acid gives the sour taste and curdles the milk. After this acid is produced in small quantity its presence proves deleterious to the growth of the bacteria, and further bacterial growth is checked. After souring, therefore, the milk for some time does not ordinarily undergo any further changes.

Milk souring has been commonly regarded as a single phenomenon, alike in all cases. When it was first studied by bacteriologists it was thought to be due in all cases to a single species of micro-organism which was discovered to be commonly present and named Bacillus acidi lactici. This bacterium has certainly the power of souring milk rapidly, and is found to be very common in dairies in Europe. As soon as bacteriologists turned their attention more closely to the subject it was found that the spontaneous souring of milk was not always caused by the same species of bacterium. Instead of finding this Bacillus acidi lactici always present, they found that quite a number of different species of bacteria have the power of souring milk, and are found in different specimens of soured milk. The number of species of bacteria which have been found to sour milk has increased until something over a hundred are known to have this power. These different species do not affect the milk in the same way. All produce some acid, but they differ in the kind and the amount of acid, and especially in the other changes which are affected at the same time that the milk is soured, so that the resulting soured milk is quite variable. In spite of this variety, however, the most recent work tends to show that the majority of cases of spontaneous souring of milk are produced by bacteria which, though somewhat variable, probably constitute a single species, and are identical with the Bacillus acidi lactici. This species, found common in the dairies of Europe, according to recent investigations occurs in this country as well. We may say, then, that while there are many species of bacteria infesting the dairy which can sour the milk, there is one which is more common and more universally found than others, and this is the ordinary cause of milk souring.

When we study more carefully the effect upon the milk of the different species of bacteria found in the dairy, we find that there is a great variety of changes which they produce when they are allowed to grow in milk. The dairyman experiences many troubles with his milk. It sometimes curdles without becoming acid. Sometimes it becomes bitter, or acquires an unpleasant "tainted" taste, or, again, a "soapy" taste. Occasionally a dairyman finds his milk becoming slimy, instead of souring and curdling in the normal fashion. At such times, after a number of hours, the milk becomes so slimy that it can be drawn into long threads. Such an infection proves very troublesome, for many a time it persists in spite of all attempts made to remedy it. Again, in other cases the milk will turn blue, acquiring about the time it becomes sour a beautiful sky-blue colour. Or it may become red, or occasionally yellow. All of these troubles the dairyman owes to the presence in his milk of unusual species of bacteria which grow there abundantly.

Excerpt from *The Story of Germ Life* by Herbert William Conn

14. Which word is most similar to *deleterious* in the first paragraph?
    a. Amicable
    b. Smoldering
    c. Luminous
    d. Ruinous

15. Which statement best describes how the passage is organized?
    a. The author begins by presenting the effects of a phenomenon, then explains the process of this phenomenon, and then ends by giving the history of the study of this phenomenon.
    b. The author begins by explaining a process or phenomenon, then gives the history of the study of this phenomenon, this ends by presenting the effects of this phenomenon.
    c. The author begins by giving the history of the study of a certain phenomenon, then explains the process of this phenomenon, then ends by presenting the effects of this phenomenon.
    d. The author begins by giving a broad definition of a subject, then presents more specific cases of the subject, then ends by contrasting two different viewpoints on the subject.

16. What is the primary purpose of the passage?
    a. To inform the reader of the phenomenon, investigation, and consequences of milk souring
    b. To persuade the reader that milk souring is due to *Bacillus acidi lactici*, found commonly in the dairies of Europe
    c. To describe the accounts and findings of researchers studying the phenomenon of milk souring
    d. To discount the former researchers' opinions on milk souring and bring light to new investigations

17. What does the author say about the ordinary cause of milk souring?
    a. Milk souring is caused mostly by a species of bacteria called *Bacillus acidi lactici*, although former research asserted that it was caused by a variety of bacteria.
    b. The ordinary cause of milk souring is unknown to current researchers, although former researchers thought it was due to a species of bacteria called *Bacillus acidi lactici*.
    c. Milk souring is caused mostly by a species of bacteria identical to that of *Bacillus acidi lactici*, although there are a variety of other bacteria that cause milk souring as well.
    d. The ordinary cause of milk souring is that milk will sometimes curdle without becoming acidic, though sometimes it will turn colors other than white, or have strange smells or tastes.

18. Which statement would the author of the passage agree with the most?
    a. Milk researchers in the past have been incompetent and have sent us on a wild goose chase when determining what causes milk souring.
    b. Dairymen are considered more expert in the field of milk souring than milk researchers.
    c. The study of milk souring has improved throughout the years, as we now understand more of what causes milk souring and what happens afterward.
    d. Any type of bacteria will turn milk sour, so it's best to keep milk in an airtight container while it is being used.

19. Which statement is the closest analogue to the author's description of what happens after milk becomes slimy?
    a. The chemical change that occurs when a firework explodes
    b. A rainstorm that overwaters a succulent plant
    c. Mercury leaking from a thermometer
    d. A child who swallows flea medication

20. Which type of paragraph would most likely come after the third paragraph?
   a. A paragraph depicting the general effects of bacteria on milk
   b. A paragraph explaining a broad history of what researchers have found out about milk souring
   c. A paragraph outlining the properties of milk souring and the way in which it occurs
   d. A paragraph showing the ways bacteria contaminate milk and how to avoid this contamination

*Questions 21–23: Complete the flow chart below with NO MORE THAN ONE WORD per answer.*

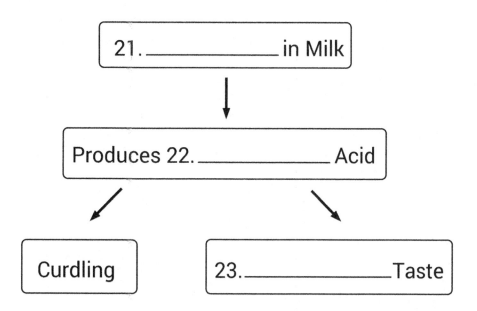

21. _____ in Milk

Produces 22. _____ Acid

Curdling

23. _____ Taste

*Questions 24–27: Match the sentences to the correct heading, **A-F**, found below.*

24. Some of the less common changes can produce . . .

25. While there are many different types of bacteria that can cause milk to sour, they are . . .

26. Milk souring was initially viewed as . . .

27. After souring, bacteria growth often plummets because . . .

A. an inevitable change which cannot be avoided.

B. the souring process involves the conversion of sugar into lactic acid.

C. closely related to *Bacillus acidi lactici*, which is by far the most common culprit.

D. when milk sours it always becomes so slimy it can be pulled out in strings.

E. shocking transformations, including color, taste, and texture changes

F. all types of bacteria that can be found only in Europe.

*Questions 28–34 are based on the following passage:*

To the Greeks and Romans, rhetoric meant the theory of oratory. As a pedagogical mechanism, it endeavored to teach students to persuade an audience. The content of rhetoric included all that the ancients had learned to be of value in persuasive public speech. It taught how to work up a case by drawing valid inferences from sound evidence, how to organize this material in the most persuasive order, and how to compose in clear and harmonious sentences. Thus, to the Greeks and Romans, rhetoric was defined by its function of discovering means to persuasion and was taught in the schools as something that every free-born man could and should learn.

In both these respects the ancients felt that poetics, the theory of poetry, was different from rhetoric. As the critical theorists believed that the poets were inspired, they endeavored less to teach men to be poets than to point out the excellences which the poets had attained. Although these critics generally, with the exceptions of Aristotle and Eratosthenes, believed the greatest value of poetry to be in the teaching of morality, no one of them endeavored to define poetry, as they did rhetoric, by its purpose. To Aristotle, and centuries later to Plutarch, the distinguishing mark of poetry was imitation. Not until the renaissance did critics define poetry as an art of imitation endeavoring to inculcate morality . . .

The same essential difference between classical rhetoric and poetics appears in the content of classical poetics. Whereas classical rhetoric deals with speeches which might be delivered to convict or acquit a defendant in the law court, or to secure a certain action by the deliberative assembly, or to adorn an occasion, classical poetic deals with lyric, epic, and drama. It is a commonplace that classical literary critics paid little attention to the lyric. It is less frequently realized that they devoted almost as little space to discussion of metrics. By far the greater bulk of classical treatises on poetics is devoted to characterization and to the technique of plot construction, involving as it does narrative and dramatic unity and movement as distinct from logical unity and movement.

*from Rhetoric and Poetry in the Renaissance: A Study of Rhetorical Terms in English Renaissance Literary Criticism by DL Clark*

28. What does the author say about one way in which the purpose of poetry changed for later philosophers?
    a. The author says that at first, poetry was not defined by its purpose but was valued for its ability to be used to teach morality. Later, some philosophers would define poetry by its ability to instill morality. Finally, during the renaissance, poetry was believed to be an imitative art, but was not necessarily believed to instill morality in its readers.
    b. The author says that the classical understanding of poetry dealt with its ability to be used to teach morality. Later, philosophers would define poetry by its ability to imitate life. Finally, during the renaissance, poetry was believed to be an imitative art that instilled morality in its readers.
    c. The author says that at first, poetry was thought to be an imitation of reality, then later, philosophers valued poetry more for its ability to instill morality.
    d. The author says that the classical understanding of poetry was that it dealt with the search for truth through its content; later, the purpose of poetry would be through its entertainment value.
    e. The author says that the initial understanding of the purpose of poetry was its entertainment value. Then, as poetry evolved into a more religious era, the renaissance, it was valued for its ability to instill morality through its teaching.

29. What does the author of the passage say about classical literary critics in relation to poetics?

a. That rhetoric was valued more than poetry because rhetoric had a definitive purpose to persuade an audience, and poetry's wavering purpose made it harder for critics to teach.

b. That although most poetry was written as lyric, epic, or drama, the critics were most focused on the techniques of lyric and epic and their performance of musicality and structure.

c. That although most poetry was written as lyric, epic, or drama, the critics were most focused on the techniques of the epic and drama and their performance of structure and character.

d. That the study of poetics was more pleasurable than the study of rhetoric due to its ability to assuage its audience, and the critics, therefore, focused on what poets did to create that effect.

e. That since poetics was made by the elite in Greek and Roman society, literary critics resented poetics for its obsession of material things and its superfluous linguistics.

30. What is the primary purpose of this passage?

a. To alert the readers to Greek and Roman culture regarding poetic texts and the focus on characterization and plot construction rather than lyric and meter.

b. To inform the readers of the changes in poetic critical theory throughout the years and to contrast those changes to the solidity of rhetoric.

c. To educate the audience on rhetoric by explaining the historical implications of using rhetoric in the education system.

d. To convince the audience that poetics is a subset of rhetoric as viewed by the Greek and Roman culture.

e. To contemplate the differences between classical rhetoric and poetry and to consider their purposes in a particular culture.

31. The word *inculcate* in the second paragraph can be best interpreted as meaning which one of the following?

a. Imbibe

b. Instill

c. Implode

d. Inquire

e. Idolize

32. Which of the following most closely resembles the way in which the passage is structured?

a. The first paragraph presents an issue. The second paragraph offers a solution to the problem. The third paragraph summarizes the first two paragraphs.

b. The first paragraph presents definitions and examples of a particular subject. The second paragraph presents a second subject in the same way. The third paragraph offers a contrast of the two subjects.

c. The first paragraph presents an inquiry. The second paragraph explains the details of that inquiry. The last paragraph offers a solution.

d. The first paragraph presents two subjects alongside definitions and examples. The second paragraph presents a comparison of the two subjects. The third paragraph presents a contrast of the two subjects.

e. The first paragraph offers a solution to a problem. The second paragraph questions the solution. The third paragraph offers a different solution.

33. Given the author's description of the content of rhetoric in the first paragraph, which one of the following is most analogous to what it taught? (The sentence is shown below.)

*It taught how to work up a case by drawing valid inferences from sound evidence, how to organize this material in the most persuasive order, how to compose in clear and harmonious sentences.*

    a. As a musician, they taught me that the end product of the music is everything—what I did to get there was irrelevant, whether it was my ability to read music or the reliance on my intuition to compose.

    b. As a detective, they taught me that time meant everything when dealing with a new case, that the simplest explanation is usually the right one, and that documentation is extremely important to credibility.

    c. As a writer, they taught me the most important thing about writing was consistently showing up to the page every single day, no matter where my muse was.

    d. As a football player, they taught me how to understand the logistics of the game, how my placement on the field affected the rest of the team, and how to run and throw with a mixture of finesse and strength.

    e. As a doctor, they taught me how to show compassion towards patients and how to take care of my own physical and mental health while running my own practice.

34. Which of the following words, if substituted for the word *treatises* in paragraph three, would LEAST change the meaning of the sentence?

    a. Thesauruses

    b. Encyclopedias

    c. Sermons

    d. Anthems

    e. Commentary

**Passage I**

*(from "Free Speech in War Time" by James Parker Hall, written in 1921, published in Columbia Law Review, Vol. 21 No. 6)*

In approaching this problem of interpretation, we may first put out of consideration certain obvious limitations upon the generality of all guaranties of free speech. An occasional unthinking malcontent may urge that the only meaning not fraught with danger to liberty is the literal one that no utterance may be forbidden, no matter what its intent or result; but in fact it is nowhere seriously argued by anyone whose opinion is entitled to respect that direct and intentional incitations to crime may not be forbidden by the state. If a state may properly forbid murder or robbery or treason, it may also punish those who induce or counsel the commission of such crimes. Any other view makes a mockery of the state's power to declare and punish offences. And what the state may do to prevent the incitement of serious crimes which are universally condemned, it may also do to prevent the incitement of lesser crimes, or of those in regard to the bad tendency of which public opinion is divided. That is, if the state may punish John for burning straw in an alley, it may also constitutionally punish Frank for inciting John to do it, though Frank did so by speech or writing. And if, in 1857, the United States could punish John for helping a fugitive slave to escape, it could also punish Frank for inducing John to do this, even though a large section of public opinion might applaud John and condemn the Fugitive Slave Law.

**Passage II**

*(from "Freedom of Speech in War Time" by Zechariah Chafee, Jr. written in 1919, published in Harvard Law Review Vol. 32 No. 8)*

The true boundary line of the First Amendment can be fixed only when Congress and the courts realize that the principle on which speech is classified as lawful or unlawful involves the balancing against each other of two very important social interests, in public safety and in the search for truth. Every reasonable attempt should be made to maintain both interests unimpaired, and the great interest in free speech should be sacrificed only when the interest in public safety is really imperiled, and not, as most men believe, when it is barely conceivable that it may be slightly affected. In war time, therefore, speech should be unrestricted by the censorship or by punishment, unless it is clearly liable to cause direct and dangerous interference with the conduct of the war.

Thus our problem of locating the boundary line of free speech is solved. It is fixed close to the point where words will give rise to unlawful acts. We cannot define the right of free speech with the precision of the Rule against Perpetuities or the Rule in Shelley's Case, because it involves national policies which are much more flexible than private property, but we can establish a workable principle of classification in this method of balancing and this broad test of certain danger. There is a similar balancing in the determination of what is "due process of law." And we can with certitude declare that the First Amendment forbids the punishment of words merely for their injurious tendencies. The history of the Amendment and the political function of free speech corroborate each other and make this conclusion plain.

*Questions 35–40: Do the statements accurately reflect the information expressed in the passages above? Answer the question with either:*

*TRUE if the statement accurately expresses the information.*

*FALSE if the statement contradicts information contained in the passages.*

*NOT GIVEN if the information contained in the statement isn't referenced in the passages.*

35. Hall believes governments should not punish people for inciting crime when the underlying law is widely unpopular.

36. Chafee argues that questionable speech should be evaluated based on a balancing test consisting of several factors.

37. Hall supports the Fugitive Slave Law as a sound public policy in addition to general support for respecting all laws.

38. Chafee asserts that wartime censorship is only appropriate when the speech is directly and dangerously harmful to the war effort.

39. Hall contends that people who incite crimes by speech or writing should be exempt from prosecution.

40. Chafee opposes the Rule against Perpetuities and the Rule in Shelley's Case as matters of law.

# Writing

**First Task**

Test takers are encouraged to spend 20 minutes on this task.

> Upon the recent hire to your dream job, you have been excited to take on any and all projects your task supervisor gives you. Lately, however, you find yourself unable to complete all the projects on time, and you feel overwhelmed with the amount of work you're being tasked with.

Prepare a letter of at least 150 words to your task supervisor. Cover the following items in your letter:

- Express your feelings about the job in general
- Reveal the struggles you are having with time management
- Request for more time to complete projects or ask for suggestions

Address information should not be included.

Begin the letter in the following way:

> Hi Linda:

**Second Task**

Write an essay of at least 250 words on the topic below:

> The evolution of the family unit has experienced many changes in the past 100 years. Many would say that the family unit has gotten weaker throughout the century and that traditional family values have gotten kicked to the wayside. Others say that a different kind of modern family has emerged, and new values have taken place of traditional values.

Write a response in which you expand on the topic above and offer your own opinion or solution on the topic. Once you've identified your stance, use concrete evidence to support your argument.

# Speaking

**Part 1**

What were your favorite and least favorite jobs?

**Part 2**

```
                    Candidate Task Card

Describe your ideal job.

Discuss when it started, how long you've participated in it, and
why you value it.

```

**Part 3**

How do you prioritize compensation and personal fulfillment when looking for a new job?

# Academic Answers

## *Listening*

**1. C:** The horizontal line at the bottom left of the diagram represents the first mile the tourist needs to walk. Number 38 is toward the end on the left, right before the tourist is supposed to head north, so it is the movie theater.

**2. D:** The big box at the end of the line is where the tourist enters when he starts heading north. So, Number 39 must be the park.

**3. B:** The smaller box is the baseball fields, and it's the halfway point to the museum. So, Number 40 must be the baseball fields.

**4. A:** The box at the top of the park is the art museum. It's where the line stops, which represents the tourist's final destination.

**5. D:** From context, we know the tourist uses "getting turned around" to describe not knowing where they are. So we can infer that "getting turned around" means becoming lost. Choices *A* and *B* aren't implied anywhere in the conversation, and the tourist has never been to the art museum, so they didn't leave their map there.

**6. C:** The tourist is repeating the directions to confirm they understand them. We know this because the tourist says, "Is that right?" after repeating the directions. The tourist doesn't ask a question about turning left or right at the movie theater. There's no evidence to support the idea that the tourist didn't hear the directions or doesn't speak English well.

**7. Mile:** The local tells the tourist to walk east for one mile.

**8. Left:** The giant movie theater is on the left, according to the transcript.

**9. Park:** Before the tourist gets to the park, they must turn left.

**10. Baseball fields:** Baseball fields are on the left before the museum.

**11. B:** Although Watson discusses an investigation, there's no evidence to support Watson running a legal practice, so Choice *F* is incorrect. In the second sentence of the second paragraph, Watson mentions his return to civil practice. Thus, Choice *B* is the correct answer.

**12. H:** At the end of the second paragraph, Watson states that several Paddington Station officials were patients. Watson cured one of these officials of a painful and lingering disease, and this former patient regularly advertised Watson's prodigious talents to his coworkers. In other words, Watson's former patients sent him referrals. Thus, Choice *H* is the correct answer.

**13. E:** Watson didn't work closely with either Hatherley or Warburton. Rather than coworkers, those were cases Watson had brought to Holmes. As such, Choice *D* and Choice *I* are both incorrect. Watson repeatedly describes how he previously worked closely with Holmes. Thus, Choice *E* is the correct answer.

**14. G:** In the first sentence of the third paragraph, Watson describes how his maid woke him up at 7 AM by tapping at the door. The maid woke Watson to tell him that two men from Paddington Station were waiting to speak with him. Thus, Choice *G* is the correct answer.

**15. C:** Watson describes Holmes as having bohemian habits, not the person he met with at 7 AM, so Choice *A* is incorrect. In the final sentence of the passage, Watson describes how the guard entered the room and closed the door behind him. Thus, Choice *C* is the correct answer.

**16. Holmes:** Watson brought two cases to *Holmes*. In the first sentence of the passage, Watson describes how many cases came to Holmes' attention, and the only two cases Watson brought to Holmes were Mr. Hatherley's thumb and Colonel Warburton's madness. Thus, *Holmes* is the correct answer.

**17. Railway:** In the second paragraph, Watson mentions he lives near Paddington Station and his practice has steadily grown based on the officials who became patients, especially after one former patient began providing referrals. In the third paragraph, Watson clarifies that Paddington Station was a railway, so his patients were railway officials. Thus, *railway* is the correct answer.

**18. Paddington:** Watson describes how he lived near Paddington Station in the second paragraph. The proximity of Paddington Station to Watson's office was a major way Watson obtained new clients. Thus, *Paddington* is the correct answer.

**19. Newspapers:** In the first paragraph, Watson states that the case of Colonel Warburton's madness had been printed in the newspapers. Watson goes on to say that newspapers' straightforward account in a single half-column of print can't do justice to the mystery, which is why he wants to tell the story. Thus, *newspapers* is the correct answer.

**20. Baker:** At the beginning of the second paragraph, Watson states that before he returned to civil practice he'd worked with Holmes in the Baker Street rooms. Holmes continued to live in the rooms because Watson visited him in the Baker Street rooms, encouraging him to drop his bohemian habits. Thus, *Baker* is the correct answer.

**21. C:** The customer comes into the store looking for an anti-aging product for the face. The customer does not initially mention vitamin A, vitamin C, or retinol (another name for vitamin A).

**22. B:** The conversation is most likely taking place in a department store. The customer asks the employee information about specific products they can purchase. While the other answer choices are possible, the most logical conclusion is that this is a department store that sells facial products to customers.

**23. A:** The customer already has face wash that contains vitamin C. They are looking for a moisturizer and don't yet know anything about retinol.

**24. A:** The employee specifically recommends a product that contains retinol, which helps with reversing aging effects.

**25. D:** Retinol produces new cells, smooths out wrinkles, and minimizes skin damage. Vitamin C works to prevent damage to skin, and retinol is used to reverse damage that has already happened to the skin.

**26. Anti-aging:** After the customer says they have a facial wash with vitamin C, the employee explains the major benefits of vitamin C. According to the employee, vitamin C prevents further damage to skin, so the primary benefit is anti-aging. Thus, *anti-aging* is the correct answer.

**27. Wrinkles:** After the employee describes the difference between vitamin A and vitamin C, the employee asks for a recommendation to get rid of *wrinkles*. Thus, *wrinkles* is the correct answer.

**28. Skin cells:** After the customer asks for something to get rid of wrinkles, the employee recommends retinol because it is an all-in-one skincare solution. Along with neutralizing dark spots and minimizing signs of damage, retinol stimulates the production of new skin cells. Thus, *skin cells* is the correct answer.

**29. Retinol:** After the customer requests a product to get rid of wrinkles, the employee suggests purchasing a product that contains retinol. According to the employee, retinol is a sort of all-in-one solution for reversing skin damage. Thus, *retinol* is the correct answer.

**30. Vitamin A:** When the customer asks if retinol is dangerous, the employee clarifies that retinol is another name for vitamin A. While vitamin C works to prevent skin damage, vitamin A works to reverse existing skin damage. Thus, *vitamin A* is the correct answer.

**31. A:** The politician's primary purpose is to outline the Nation's future plans. He is identifying problems and then proposing a series of regulations as the solution. The speech does mention the "evils of the old order," but this criticism of past policies and enemies serves the primary purpose of outlining his plans. The politician calls for supporting agriculture, but it's also part of the larger agenda he's outlining.

**32. D:** Early in the speech, the politician says, "Our greatest primary task is to put people to work." The rest of the choices are part of the broader political agenda, but they're not identified as the greatest primary task.

**33. D:** It can be inferred that the economy is in a depression. The politician proposes what seems to be a radical agenda, one that's far different from what came before. In the opening paragraph, he mentions how the nation "will endure...and revive" once they stop living in fear. All this is describing an economic crisis that is much closer to a depression than the other choices.

**34. C:** The politician calls for "engaging on a national scale in a redistribution... to provide a better use of the land for those best fitted for the land." And then he later argues for an "end to speculation with other people's money" and a sound currency. A lack of natural resources is never identified as a problem.

**35. B:** The politician compares rescuing the economy with fighting a war. He concludes the speech with his request to Congress for "broad Executive power to wage a war against the emergency." The other answer choices identify actions the politician wants to take to rescue the economy, but they aren't part of an analogy.

**36. D:** The flowchart is about the politician's plans to address the economic depression. Although the politician states his desire for broad reform to the banking system, he doesn't mention banking power. Furthermore, the politician's plans and the third row of boxes is much more broad than just banking, so Choice *A* is incorrect. In the final paragraph, the politician lays out his plans to obtain broad executive power. Without broad executive power, the politician wouldn't be able to implement his sweeping reforms, which are outlined in the third row of boxes. Thus, Choice *D* is the correct answer.

**37. E:** The correct answer will be something the politician wants to redistribute. While the politician would probably favor resource redistribution, this isn't mentioned in the passage. In addition, "Resources Redistribution" doesn't make grammatical sense, so Choice *F* is incorrect. Likewise, the politician wants to ensure the currency is adequate and sound, but he doesn't mention redistributing currency. So, Choice *B* is incorrect. In the third paragraph, the politician describes his plan to redistribute land in order to maximize efficient land use practices. Thus, Choice *E* is the correct answer.

**38. C:** In the second paragraph, the politician claims his primary task is to put people to work. According to the politician, the government can increase employment to complete vital projects, such as the reorganization of natural resources. Thus, Choice *C* is the correct answer.

**39. Fear:** In the first paragraph, the politician says the only thing people have to fear is fear itself. According to the politician, if people don't first face this fear, they will be unable to make the efforts needed for progress. Thus, *fear* is the correct answer.

**40. Congress:** In the last paragraph, the politician demands that Congress needs to act. If Congress fails to act, the politician declares he will treat the economic depression as a war-like emergency, meaning the politician will unilaterally seize the broad executive power he'd previously requested from Congress. Thus, *Congress* is the correct answer.

# *Reading*

**1. D:** The report is mostly objective; its language does not display any strong emotion whatsoever. The story is told as an objective documentation of a sequence of actions: we see the president sitting in his box with his wife, their enjoyment of the show, Booth's walk through the crowd to the box, and Ford's consideration of Booth's movements. There is perhaps a small amount of bias when the author mentions the president's "worthy wife." However, the word choice and style show no signs of excitement, sadness, anger, or apprehension from the author's perspective, so the best answer is Choice *D*.

**2. B:** Mr. Ford assumed Booth's movement throughout the theater was due to Booth's familiarity with the events of the theater. Choice *A* is incorrect; although Booth does eventually make his way to Lincoln's box, Mr. Ford does not make this observation in this part of the passage. Choice *C* is incorrect; although the passage mentions "companions," it mentions Lincoln's companions rather than Booth's companions. Choice *D* is incorrect; the passage mentions "dress circle," which means the first level of the theater, but this is different from a "dressing room."

**3. C:** The lead singer, like the actor Mr. Sothern, is very significant and the singer's exit leaves the band worse off. In the passage, Mr. Sothern leaves the theater company, and then the play becomes a "very dull affair." Choice *A* depicts a dancer who backs out of an event before the final performance, so this is incorrect. Choice *B* describes a ballerina who makes it into Julliard but is expelled due to criminal activity. This is not the correct answer, as the ballerina's departure does not harm the school in this answer choice. Choice *D* is incorrect. The actor departs an event, but there is no assessment of the quality of the movie.

**4. A:** It's tempting to mark Choice *A* wrong because the genres are different. Choice *A* is a fictional text, and the original passage is not a fictional account. However, the question asks specifically for organizational structure. Choice *A* is organized as a chronological structure just like the passage, so this is the correct answer. The passage does not have a cause-and-effect structure or problem-solution structure, making Choices *B* and *D* incorrect. Choice *C* is tempting because it mentions an autobiography; however, the structure of this text starts at the end and works its way back to the beginning, which is the opposite structure of the original passage.

**5. C:** The word *adornment* would LEAST change the meaning of the sentence because it's the most closely related word to *festoons*. The other choices don't make sense in the context of the sentence. *Feathers, armies,* and *buckets* are not as accurate in this context as the word *adornments*. The passage also talks about other décor in the setting, so the word *adornments* fits right in with the context of the paragraph.

**6. D:** Choice *A* is incorrect; the author makes no claims and uses no rhetoric of persuasion on the audience. Choice *B* is incorrect, though it's a tempting choice; the passage depicts the setting in exorbitant detail, but the setting itself is not the primary purpose of the passage. Choice *C* is incorrect; one could argue this is a narrative, and the passage is about Lincoln's last few hours, but this isn't the *best* choice. The best choice recounts the details that leads up to Lincoln's death.

**7. Front Door:** The fifth paragraph describes how Booth walked back out the stable door and came around the theater to enter through the front door.

**8. Dress circle:** In the first paragraph, the dress circle and box are described as being above and to the side of the stage.

**9. C:** Section I is a description of the theater's boxes. Amongst other information, this section describes the number of boxes, and their locations, entrances, and décor. Thus, Choice *C* is the correct answer.

**10. F:** Section II describes the presidential seating arrangement in the box. The section describes President Lincoln's armchair and its position relative to the seats of Mrs. Lincoln, Miss Harris, and Major Rathbone. In addition, Section II states the total number of people seated in the presidential box. Thus, Choice *F* is the correct answer.

**11. A:** Section III describes the audience's reaction to the play *Our American Cousin*. While the author describes the play as a "very dull affair" without the acting talent of Mr. Southern, it still elicited an incredibly positive reaction from the audience. In particular, Mrs. Lincoln watched the play with "amused attention," and a smile even broke President Lincoln's "habitual sadness." Therefore, *Our American Cousin* was a crowd-pleasing act and Choice *A* is the correct answer.

**12: G:** Section IV provides information about the stable, which was located in the rear of the theater. Specifically, the stable housed a horse that had been given exquisite care. Although this section mentions the entrance of a young man that we later learn is Booth, the bulk of this section is about the location and contents of the stable. Thus, Choice *G* is the correct answer.

**13: E:** Although Section V is the only section to mention Mr. Ford, the owner of the theater, it doesn't mention his departure. As such, Choice *H* is incorrect. Likewise, this section doesn't describe the final act of the play, so Choice *D* is incorrect. Instead, the focus of Section V is Mr. Booth's entrance into the theater and the path he took toward President Lincoln's box. Thus, Choice *E* is the correct answer.

**14. D:** The word *deleterious* can be best interpreted as similar to the word *ruinous*. The first paragraph explains that bacteria in souring milk produce lactic acid, and that the acid soon prevents more bacteria from growing. Therefore the acid has a ruinous effect on the bacteria. Choice *A*, *amicable*, means friendly, so this does not make sense in context. Choice *B*, *smoldering*, means to burn without flame, so this is also incorrect. Choice *C*, luminous, means shining or brilliant and doesn't make sense in the context of the passage.

**15. B:** The author explains the process of souring in the first paragraph by informing the reader that "it is due to the action of certain of the milk bacteria." In paragraph two, the author explains how the phenomenon of milk souring was viewed when it was first studied, and then toward the end of the paragraph the author gives his insight into "recent investigations." Finally, the passage ends by presenting the effects of the phenomenon of milk souring. All the other answer choices are incorrect.

**16: A:** Choice *B* is incorrect because the passage states that *Bacillus acidi lactici* is not the only cause of milk souring. Choice *C* is incorrect because, although the author mentions the findings of researchers, the main purpose of the text is not to describe their accounts and findings, as we are not even told the names of any of the researchers. Choice *D* is tricky. The author present new findings in contrast to the first cases studied by researchers. However, this information is only in the second paragraph, so it is not the primary purpose of the *entire passage*.

**17. C:** Milk souring is caused mostly by a species of bacteria identical to that of *Bacillus acidi lactici*, although a variety of other bacteria also cause milk to sour. Choice *A* is incorrect because it contradicts the assertion that the souring is still caused by a variety of bacteria. Choice *B* is incorrect because the ordinary cause of milk souring *is known* to current researchers. Choice *D* is incorrect because it describes the effects of milk souring, not the cause.

**18. C:** None of the choices here are explicitly stated in the passage, so answering the question requires making inferences. Choice *A* is incorrect because there is no indication from the author that milk researchers in the past have been incompetent, only that recent research has done a better job of studying the phenomenon of milk souring. Choice *B* is incorrect because the author refers to dairymen but does not compare them to milk researchers. Choice *D* is incorrect because we are told in the second paragraph that only certain types of bacteria can cause milk to sour. Choice *C* is the best answer choice here because, although the author does not directly state that the study of milk souring has improved, we can see this is true due to the comparison of old studies to newer studies, and the fact that the newer studies are being used as a reference in the passage.

**19. A:** The author tells us that after milk becomes slimy, "it persists in spite of all attempts made to remedy it," which means the milk has gone through a chemical change. It has changed its state from milk to sour milk by changing its odor, color, and material. After a firework explodes, there is nothing one can do to change the substance of a firework back to its original form; the original substance is turned into sound and light. Choice *B* is incorrect because, although the rain overwatered the plant, it's possible that the plant will recover from this. Choice *C* is incorrect because although mercury leaking out may be dangerous, the actual substance itself stays the same. Choice *D* is incorrect; this situation is not analogous to the alteration of a substance.

**20. D:** Choices *A, B,* and *C* are incorrect because these are already represented in the third, second, and first paragraphs. Choice *D* is the best answer because it follows a sort of problem/solution structure in writing.

**21. Bacteria:** The first row of boxes in the flowchart shows the beginning of a process, and the passage primarily focuses on how bacteria causes milk to sour. The other two rows of boxes confirm that the flowchart is specifically about the process by which milk sours. According to the passage, bacteria in milk causes the milk to go sour. Thus, *bacteria* is the correct answer.

**22. Lactic:** The second row of boxes in this flowchart causes the effects listed in the third row. The passage explains how bacteria in milk converts sugar into lactic acid, and the lactic acid causes the milk to curdle and taste sour. Thus, *lactic* is the correct answer.

**23. Sour:** The third row of boxes is the final step in the process of milk souring. According to the first paragraph of the passage, after bacteria in milk produces lactic acid through its interaction with sugar, it leads to the milk curdling and developing a sour taste. Thus, *sour* is the correct answer.

**24. E:** The last paragraph describes some of the less common changes bacteria can cause in milk. Rather than simply souring and curdling the milk, which occurs in the overwhelming majority of cases, bacteria can sometimes create a soapy taste and turn the milk into slimy string. Additionally, in some rare cases, bacteria can turn the milk red, blue, or yellow. Thus, Choice *E* is the correct answer.

**25. C:** The second paragraph describes how different types of bacteria can trigger the souring process in milk. Despite the great variety of bacteria, the passage concludes that all of these species of bacteria are nearly identical to *Bacillus acidi lactici*. The second paragraph states that *Bacillus acidi lactici* can be found all across Europe, but it doesn't claim that this bacteria can only be found in Europe. As such, Choice *F* is incorrect. Thus, Choice *C* is the correct answer.

**26. A:** The second sentence of the first paragraph describes how people originally viewed the souring of milk. Prior to the discovery of bacteria's role in the souring of milk, people considered souring to be an inherent property of milk. Thus, Choice *A* is the correct answer.

**27. B:** At the end of the first paragraph, the author describes what happens to bacteria growth during the souring process. According to the passage, bacteria converts sugar into lactic acid, and the acidic environment halts the bacteria's growth. Although Choice *D* completes the sentence grammatically, it doesn't do so logically. The souring process only turns the milk into slimy string under relatively rare circumstances, and in any event, this phenomenon isn't an impediment to the bacteria's growth. Lactic acid is directly related to curbing the growth of bacteria. Thus, Choice *B* is the correct answer.

**28. B:** The author says that the classical understanding of poetry dealt with its ability to be used to teach morality. Later, philosophers would define poetry by its ability to imitate life. Finally, during the renaissance, poetry was believed to be an imitative art that instilled morality in its readers. The rest of the answer choices improperly interpret this explanation in the passage. Poetry was never mentioned for use in entertainment, which makes Choices *D* and *E* incorrect. Choices *A* and *C* are incorrect because they mix up the chronological order.

**29. C:** The author says that although most poetry was written as lyric, epic, or drama, the critics were most focused on the techniques of the epic and drama and their performance of structure and character. This is the best answer choice as portrayed by paragraph three. Choice *A* is incorrect because nowhere in the passage does it say rhetoric was more valued than poetry, although it did seem to have a more definitive purpose than poetry. Choice *B* is incorrect; this almost mirrors Choice *A*, but the critics were *not* focused on the lyric, as the passage indicates. Choice *D* is incorrect because the passage does not mention that the study of poetics was more pleasurable than the study of rhetoric. Choice *E* is incorrect because again, we do not see anywhere in the passage where poetry was reserved for the most elite in society.

**30. E:** The purpose is to contemplate the differences between classical rhetoric and poetry and to consider their purposes in a particular culture. Choice *A* is incorrect; this thought is discussed in the third paragraph, but it is not the main idea of the passage. Choice *B* is incorrect; although changes in poetics throughout the years is mentioned, this is not the main idea of the passage. Choice *C* is incorrect; although this is partly true—that rhetoric within the education system is mentioned—the subject of poetics is left out of this answer choice. Choice *D* is incorrect; the passage makes no mention of poetics being a subset of rhetoric.

**31. B:** The correct answer choice is Choice *B*, *instill*. Choice *A*, *imbibe*, means to drink heavily, so this choice is incorrect. Choice *C*, *implode*, means to collapse inward, which does not make sense in this context. Choice *D*, *inquire*, means to investigate. This option is better than the other options, but it is not as accurate as *instill*. Choice *E*, *idolize*, means to admire, which does not make sense in this context.

**32. B:** The first paragraph presents definitions and examples of a particular subject. The second paragraph presents a second subject in the same way. The third paragraph offers a contrast of the two subjects. In the passage, we see the first paragraph defining rhetoric and offering examples of how the Greeks and Romans taught this subject. In the second paragraph, poetics is defined and examples of its dynamic definition are provided. In the third paragraph, the contrast between rhetoric and poetry is characterized through how each of these were studied in a classical context.

**33. D:** The best answer is Choice *D:* As a football player, they taught me how to understand the logistics of the game, how my placement on the field affected the rest of the team, and how to run and throw with a mixture of finesse and strength. The content of rhetoric in the passage . . . "taught how to work up a case by drawing valid inferences from sound evidence, how to organize this material in the most persuasive order, and how to compose in clear and harmonious sentences. What we have here is three general principles: 1) it taught me how to understand logic and reason (drawing inferences parallels to understanding the logistics of the game), 2) it taught me how to understand structure and organization (organization of material parallels to organization on the field) and 3) it taught me how to make the end product beautiful (how to compose in harmonious sentences parallels to how to run with finesse and strength). Each part parallels by logic, organization, and style.

**34. E:** *Treatises* is most closely related to the word *commentary.* Choices *A* and *B* do not make sense because thesauruses and encyclopedias are not written about one single subject. Choice *C* is incorrect; sermons are usually given by religious leaders as advice or teachings. Choice *D* is incorrect; anthems are songs and do not fit within the context of this sentence.

**35. False:** The author of Passage I, Hall, takes the position that the United States should prosecute people for incitements to crime regardless of public opinion about the underlying law. In the middle of the passage, Hall argues that the United States enjoys the authority to prohibit the incitement of crimes, even when public opinion is divided over the law about the crime. Furthermore, at the end of the passage, Hall defends the United States' prosecution of people for inciting the violation of the Fugitive Slave Law, despite the fact that many people opposed the Fugitive Slave Law.

**36. True:** The author of Passage II, Chafee, argues that freedom of speech issues should be evaluated based on a balancing test. In the first paragraph, Chafee proposes that the factors involved in this balancing test are public safety and the search for truth. For example, Chafee believes the freedom of speech should remain fully protected in wartime unless the speech poses a direct danger to the war effort. Thus, *True* is the correct answer.

**37. Not Given:** At the end of the passage, Hall mentions the Fugitive Slave Law to present a scenario in which the United States enjoyed the authority to enforce a widely unpopular law. Nowhere in the passage does Chafee give an opinion on the effectiveness or reasonableness of the Fugitive Slave Law as a matter of public policy. Instead, Chafee merely uses the Fugitive Slave Law to demonstrate his general support for respecting all laws. As such, Chafee doesn't support or condemn the substantive aspects of the law. Thus, *Not Given* is the correct answer.

**38. True:** At the end of the second paragraph, Chafee applies his balancing test to war time. Specifically, Chafee balances the threat to public safety with the value of allowing people to search for truth. During war time, Chafee is opposed to restricting and censoring speech unless the speech will directly and dangerously interfere with the conduct of war. Thus, *True* is the correct answer.

**39. False:** The passage directly contradicts the statement. Hall adamantly defends the United States' authority to prosecute speech that incites criminal activity, and the passage doesn't list any exemptions for speech or writing. Near the end of the passage, Hall proposes a hypothetical in which the government has constitutional authority to punish someone for inciting a crime by speech or writing. Thus, *False* is the correct answer.

**40. Not Given:** Chafee mentions the Rule against Perpetuities and the Rule in Shelley's Case as examples of unambiguous legal principles to contrast with his fluid balancing test for the freedom of speech. Since Chafee doesn't otherwise discuss the Rule against Perpetuities and the Rule in Shelley's Case, it's unclear whether he supports or opposes these legal principles. Thus, *Not Given* is the correct answer.

# Academic Listening Transcripts

## Passage #1: Tourist Conversation

**(Narrator)** Listen to the conversation between the local and the tourist and then answer the questions.

**(Tourist)** Excuse me, ma'am, do you have a second?

**(Local)** Sure. What's up?

**(Tourist)** I'm trying to find the art museum, but I keep getting turned around. At this point I'm not even sure where I am. Would you be able to point me in the right direction?

**(Local)** Of course! First, you need to walk east for about one mile. You'll know you're close when you see a giant movie theater on your left. You can't miss it. As soon as you get past the movie theater, you will see a park ahead on the corner. Turn left before getting to the park. Down the road, you'll see some baseball fields on your left. The museum is located at the most northern end of the road.

**(Tourist)** Okay so I walk east for one mile, take the left after the giant movie theater, and head north until I hit the museum. Is that right?

**(Local)** You got it.

**(Tourist)** Oh thanks so much.

**(Local)** Anytime.

## Passage #2: Actor's Monologue

**(Narrator)** Listen to the actor's monologue and then answer the questions.

Watson: Of all the problems which have been submitted to my friend, Mr. Sherlock Holmes, for solution during the years of our intimacy, there were only two which I was the means of introducing to his notice—that of Mr. Hatherley's thumb, and that of Colonel Warburton's madness. Of these the latter may have afforded a finer field for an acute and original observer, but the other was so strange in its inception and so dramatic in its details that it may be the more worthy of being placed upon record, even if it gave my friend fewer openings for those deductive methods of reasoning by which he achieved such remarkable results. The story has, I believe, been told more than once in the newspapers, but, like all such narratives, its effect is much less striking when set forth *en bloc* in a single half-column of print than when the facts slowly evolve before your own eyes, and the mystery clears gradually away as each new discovery furnishes a step which leads on to the complete truth. At the time the circumstances made a deep impression upon me, and the lapse of two years has hardly served to weaken the effect.

It was in the summer of '89, not long after my marriage, that the events occurred which I am now about to summarise. I had returned to civil practice and had finally abandoned Holmes in his Baker Street rooms, although I continually visited him and occasionally even persuaded him to forgo his Bohemian habits so far as to come and visit us. My practice had steadily increased, and as I happened to live at no very great distance from Paddington Station, I got a few patients from among the officials. One of these, whom I had cured of a painful and a lingering disease, was never weary of advertising my virtues and of endeavouring to send to me every sufferer over whom he might have any influence.

One morning, at a little before seven o'clock, I was awakened by the maid tapping at the door to announce that two men had come from Paddington and were waiting in the consulting-room. I dressed hurriedly, for I knew by experience that railway cases were seldom trivial, and hastened downstairs. As I descended, my old ally, the guard, came out of the room and closed the door tightly behind him.

## Passage #3: Customer and Employee Conversation

(Narrator) Listen to the conversation between a customer and an employee and then answer the questions.

(Customer) Excuse me, I'm looking for a good-quality anti-aging cream for sensitive skin. Can you help me find something?

(Employee) Sure! Are you looking for a facial wash or a moisturizer?

(Customer) A moisturizer; I already have a facial wash. It's one of those that has extra Vitamin C in it.

(Employee) Oh, that's good! Vitamin C will help prevent any further damage to your skin, which is great for anti-aging. Can I recommend something with retinol in it?

(Customer) That sounds dangerous. Isn't retinol some kind of chemical?

(Employee) No, not at all! Retinol is just another name for Vitamin A. Vitamin C will prevent damage, and Vitamin A will work to reverse the skin damage that you already have.

(Customer) Oh, awesome! I also want something to get rid of my wrinkles. What would you recommend I try for that?

(Employee) Actually, you're in luck! Retinol is sort of an all-in-one when it comes to reversing skin damage; it encourages production of new skin cells, neutralizes dark or multicolored spots, and minimizes any other signs of skin damage.

(Customer) Oh, perfect! I'll take some moisturizer with retinol in it, then! Thank you so much for your help!

## Passage #4: Politician's Speech

(Narrator) Listen to the politician's speech and then answer the questions.

(Politician) This is preeminently the time to speak the truth, the whole truth, frankly and boldly. We mustn't shrink from honestly facing conditions in our country today. This great Nation will endure as it has endured, will thrive and will prosper. So, first of all, let me assert my firm belief that the only thing we have to fear is fear itself—nameless, unreasoning, unjustified terror which paralyzes needed efforts to convert retreat into advance.

Our greatest primary task is to put people to work. This is no unsolvable problem if we face it wisely and courageously. It can be accomplished in part by direct recruiting by the Government itself, treating the task as we would treat the emergency of a war, but at the same time, through this employment, accomplishing greatly needed projects to stimulate and reorganize the use of our natural resources.

Hand in hand with this we must frankly recognize the overbalance of population in our industrial centers and, by engaging on a national scale in redistribution, endeavor to provide a better use of the land for those best fitted for the land. The task can be helped by definite efforts to raise the values of agricultural products and with this the power to purchase the output of our cities. It can be helped by preventing realistically the tragedy of the growing loss through the foreclosure of our small homes and our farms.

Finally, in our progress toward a resumption of work we require two safeguards against a return of the evils of the old order; there must be a strict supervision of all banking and credits and investments; there must be an end to speculation with other people's money, and there must be provision for an adequate but sound currency.

In the event that the Congress shall fail to take one of these two courses, and in the event that the national emergency is still critical, I shall not evade the clear course of duty that will then confront me. I shall ask the Congress for the one remaining instrument to meet the crisis—broad Executive power to wage a war against the emergency, as great as the power that would be given to me if we were in fact invaded by a foreign foe.

Greetings!

First, we would like to give a huge "thank you" for choosing us and this study guide for your IELTS exam. We hope that it will lead you to success on this exam and for your years to come.

Our team has tried to make your preparations as thorough as possible by covering all of the topics you should be expected to know. In addition, our writers attempted to create practice questions identical to what you will see on the day of your actual test. We have also included many test-taking strategies to help you learn the material, maintain the knowledge, and take the test with confidence.

We strive for excellence in our products, and if you have any comments or concerns over the quality of something in this study guide, please send us an email so that we may improve.

As you continue forward in life, we would like to remain alongside you with other books and study guides in our library, such as:


*GRE:* amazon.com/dp/1628457082

*LSAT:* amazon.com/dp/1628459441


We are continually producing and updating study guides in several different subjects. If you are looking for something in particular, all of our products are available on Amazon. You may also send us an email!

Sincerely,
APEX Test Prep
info@apexprep.com

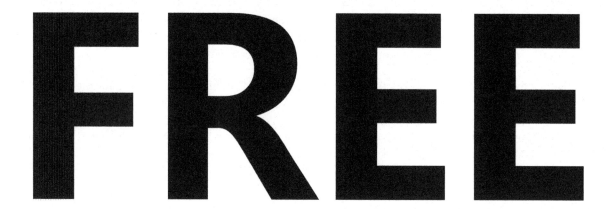

## Free Study Tips DVD

In addition to the tips and content in this guide, we have created a FREE DVD with helpful study tips to further assist your exam preparation. **This FREE Study Tips DVD provides you with top-notch tips to conquer your exam and reach your goals.**

Our simple request in exchange for the strategy-packed DVD is that you email us your feedback about our study guide. We would love to hear what you thought about the guide, and we welcome any and all feedback—positive, negative, or neutral. It is our #1 goal to provide you with top quality products and customer service.

To receive your **FREE Study Tips DVD**, email freedvd@apexprep.com. Please put "FREE DVD" in the subject line and put the following in the email:

      a. The name of the study guide you purchased.

      b. Your rating of the study guide on a scale of 1-5, with 5 being the highest score.

      c. Any thoughts or feedback about your study guide.

      d. Your first and last name and your mailing address, so we know where to send your free DVD!

Thank you!

Made in the USA
Las Vegas, NV
23 September 2021